The Open University

A first level interdisciplinary course

Using **Mathematics**

CHAPTER C1

BLOCK C
CONTINUOUS MODELS

Differentiation and modelling

Prepared by the course team

About this course

This course, MST121 *Using Mathematics*, and the courses MU120 *Open Mathematics* and MS221 *Exploring Mathematics* provide a flexible means of entry to university-level mathematics. Further details may be obtained from the Central Enquiry Service (see address below).

MST121 uses the software program Mathcad (MathSoft, Inc.) and other software to investigate mathematical and statistical concepts and as a tool in problem solving. This software is provided as part of the course, and its use is covered in the associated Computer Book.

The Open University, Walton Hall, Milton Keynes, MK7 6AA.

First published 1997. Reprinted 1997

Edited, designed and typeset by the Open University using the Open University TeX System.

Printed in the United Kingdom by Caligraving Limited, Thetford, Norfolk.

ISBN 0 7492 7860 9

This text forms part of an Open University First Level Course. If you would like a copy of *Studying with The Open University*, please write to the Central Enquiry Service, PO Box 200, The Open University, Walton Hall, Milton Keynes, MK7 6YZ. If you have not already enrolled on the Course and would like to buy this or other Open University material, please write to Open University Educational Enterprises Ltd, 12 Cofferidge Close, Stony Stratford, Milton Keynes, MK11 1BY, United Kingdom.

1.2

Contents

ground

one

Introduction to Block C

In much of Block B you used ideas from discrete mathematics, such as recurrence relations and sequences, to model phenomena that involve change. In Block C you will again be modelling change, but this time the concepts are drawn principally from continuous mathematics. Several of these concepts will be introduced as the block progresses, but there are some which you have met already. Two important ones, applying to continuous as well as to discrete mathematics, are:

◇ the description of a relationship between two quantities in the form of an equation;

◇ the visualisation of the relationship between two quantities as a graph.

See, for example, Chapter A4. You may like to refresh your memory on these points before going further with the block.

This block discusses change in cases where the change is continuous or can be modelled as being so. It addresses questions such as the following: How fast is something changing? Is it increasing or decreasing? Does it ever stop changing, permanently or temporarily? How does the change accumulate? How can the change be described by an equation?

Chapter C1 concerns the rate at which variables change, whether the change is an increase or decrease and whether the change stops. You will see a mathematical process called *differentiation* introduced to help in analysing these matters, together with illustrations of its practical applications.

Chapter C2 takes a different view towards change. Firstly the process of *integration* is introduced, as the inverse process of differentiation. You will see that integration is needed in order to solve a new type of equation, called a *differential equation*, which arises frequently in mathematical models of phenomena which change. Secondly, you will find that the importance of integration extends well beyond being the inverse of differentiation. It allows an accumulation of continuous changes to be described, and one significant application is to the finding of areas beneath graphs.

The third and final chapter of Block C discusses how appropriate functions can be chosen during the mathematical modelling process. Ideas introduced both in the previous chapters and in earlier blocks are reviewed and brought together in this discussion.

In terms of study time, Chapters C1 and C2 are of about the same length, but Chapter C3 is shorter.

The branch of mathematics which includes the study of differentiation and integration is called **calculus** and so Block C provides an introduction to calculus. The history of this branch of mathematics goes back to the second half of the seventeenth century, when Sir Isaac Newton (1642–1727) in England and Gottfried Wilhelm Leibniz (1646–1717) in what is now Germany both developed independently the basic ideas of calculus. The word 'calculus' here means 'a systematic method for solving a certain type of problem', and what Newton and Leibniz did was not so much to discover the basic ideas as to bring them together in a systematic way and then show how their systematic methods could be used to solve problems.

The Latin word *calculus* means a stone. The link is in the use of stones for counting.

Unfortunately, a bitter argument grew up over who was the first to 'discover' calculus. This split the mathematicians of the day (and for decades afterwards) into two camps and hindered the development of the subject. In fact, one legacy of the dispute is still with us: there are several notations in current use for expressing exactly the same thing in calculus. One set of notations can be traced back to Newton's work and another to that of Leibniz. Other notations arose from more recent attempts to 'tidy up' the subject, following on from the greater understanding of calculus and its associated ideas that has developed since the time of Newton and Leibniz. Technologists and scientists tend to use some of these notations, while mathematicians tend to use others. In fact, scientists and technologists from one branch of their subject may prefer to use a different notation from those in another branch.

What all of this means is that, whether you see yourself primarily as a budding mathematician, scientist or technologist, you need to recognise, understand and occasionally use all of these notations, even though you will probably settle eventually for using mainly the notation of your preferred subject area. This block therefore makes a deliberate attempt to encourage you to recognise and use a variety of current notations.

The fact that so many branches of mathematics, science and technology have drawn upon calculus is an indication of the importance and usefulness of this body of knowledge and methods. The chapters of this block refer to quite a wide range of contexts in order to illustrate the applications of calculus. As you study, you may find it useful to pause occasionally and think about the range of situations and types of problem to which calculus is applied.

Activity 0.1   *Discrete or continuous*

As you work through Block C compare the problems tackled with those in Block B, where discrete mathematics was used. Consider how they differ and note any ideas about these differences in your learning file. You may wish to use Learning File Sheet 1 for this purpose.

Study guide

This chapter is longer than average, and you should schedule six study sessions for your work on it. In the second of these you will need access to a video-cassette player, while the third and sixth require use of the computer.

The study pattern which we recommend is as follows.

Study session 1: Section 1.

Study session 2: Section 2. You will need access to your video-cassette player for the last part of this session (Subsection 2.4).

Study session 3: Section 3. You will need access to your computer for almost all of this session, together with the Mathcad disk for Block C and Computer Book C.

Study session 4: Section 4.

Study session 5: Subsections 5.1 and 5.2.

Study session 6: Subsections 5.3 to 5.5. You will need access to your computer for Subsection 5.3 together with Computer Book C. However, there are no Mathcad files associated with this session.

An alternative pattern for the last two sessions would be to study Subsections 5.1, 5.3 and 5.4 in study session 5 and Subsections 5.2 and 5.5 in study session 6. This places the computing activity in session 5 rather than in session 6. It also groups those parts of Section 5 which concentrate on the mathematics in the earlier session, and leaves for the later session those subsections which focus on some modelling applications.

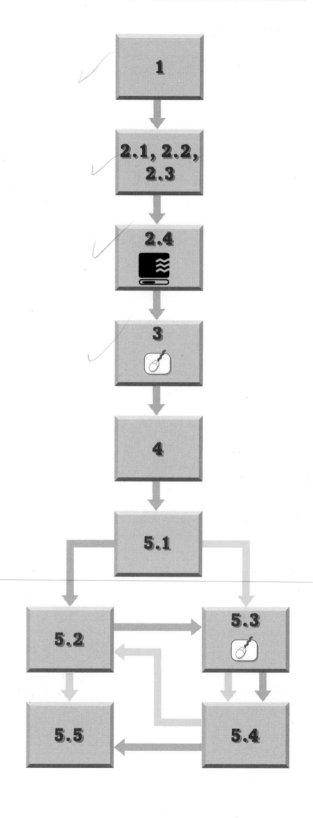

Introduction

This chapter introduces an important topic in calculus called *differentiation*. If two variables are related to each other, then differentiation permits us to describe precisely the rate at which one variable alters with respect to changes in the other. By the end of the chapter you should have a grasp of what this process means, how it is carried out and in what modelling situations it may be useful.

The first section of the chapter 'sets the scene' with an informal introduction to rates of change. Section 2 develops a more formal approach to differentiation. The aim of these two sections taken together is to give you an understanding of what differentiation is.

Section 3 then shows you how the process of differentiation is carried out, both 'by hand' and with the aid of Mathcad. The aim of this section is to enable you to carry out differentiation with some confidence.

In Sections 4 and 5, differentiation is used in the context of modelling. Two principal uses are illustrated: finding instantaneous rates of change in Section 4, and optimisation in Section 5. These two sections aim to help you to recognise situations where differentiation can be useful, to carry out the differentiations required and to interpret the results appropriately.

The learning skills themes in this chapter amount to reinforcement of themes which you have seen before. They include identifying terms which have a special mathematical meaning different from their everyday English usage, reflecting on what you are learning in order to make sense of it and finding strategies for clarifying points which are unclear to you.

1 Rates of change

To study this section, you may need a calculator.

This section introduces the topic of rates of change in an informal way, building up some basic ideas through various illustrations. A more formal approach is left until later in the chapter.

The properties of straight lines, including slope, were investigated in Chapter A3, Section 3.

Rates of change are closely associated with the *gradients* or slopes of straight lines. This is the starting point adopted in Subsection 1.1, which concentrates on laying some conceptual foundations. Then, in Subsection 1.2, you will see an example which demonstrates how instantaneous rates of change may be of interest, and how they might be calculated.

Throughout Section 1, do not worry if you find that you are not following fully every detail of the text. Concentrate rather on making out the general picture here, and leave a fuller understanding to the rest of the chapter. In fact, you might find it useful to read Section 1 again after you have studied the rest of the chapter. At that stage it should help to reinforce the ideas which you will have met in the other sections.

1.1 Some basic ideas

Gradients of curves

The word 'gradient' is an alternative term for 'slope', and will be used in this chapter.

You have seen previously that a straight line, like the one shown in Figure 1.1(a), has a slope or **gradient**, given by the formula

$$\text{gradient} = \frac{\text{increase in } y}{\text{corresponding increase in } x} \left(= \frac{\text{rise}}{\text{run}} \right).$$

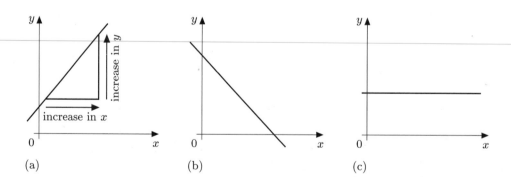

Figure 1.1

You may recall that the gradient of a straight line is the same no matter which pair of points on the line are chosen to calculate the ratio from the formula above. We say, therefore, that a straight line has constant gradient. The value of the gradient for the line in Figure 1.1(a) is positive, since y increases as x increases. A line which slopes downwards from left to right, like the one in Figure 1.1(b), has a negative gradient because y *decreases* as x increases. The horizontal straight line in Figure 1.1(c) has a gradient of zero, because y remains constant as x changes.

How can this idea of gradient be carried over to the graph of a curve, such as that shown in Figure 1.2(a)? It is possible to take any pair of points on the curve and to calculate the corresponding 'rise over run' ratio but, unlike the case with straight lines, different ratio values then arise from different pairs of points. This shows that a curve, when taken as a whole, does not have a single gradient associated with it in the way that a straight line does.

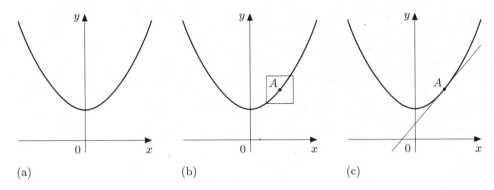

(a)   (b)   (c)

Figure 1.2

However, we can attach a meaning to the gradient of a curve *at any particular point on the curve*. To see why this is so, consider the point A marked on the graph in Figure 1.2(b), and the portion of the graph within the small rectangle which contains A. This portion of the graph, when taken on its own, looks much 'straighter' than the original, and this will be true even if the scale of the picture is adjusted so that the size of the chosen portion is enlarged to fill the space occupied by the original graph. If necessary, this 'zooming' process can be repeated several times, until the graph of the resulting reduced portion of the curve looks indistinguishable from part of a straight line through A.

This process can actually be carried out with Mathcad, using the Zoom facility.

Indeed, this straight line can be identified as the *tangent* to the curve at the point A (see Figure 1.2(c)), that is, the unique line which passes through the point A and just touches the curve at this point.

The word 'tangent' comes from the Latin verb *tangere*, meaning to touch.

For this line there is a gradient defined, and we may regard its value as being also the gradient of the original graph at A. In this block we are interested in continuous graphs which are 'locally straight' in the manner just described. Such graphs (and the functions associated with them) are said to be *smooth*. The graph of a smooth function has a gradient associated with every point on it.

Imagine now that the point A is moved along the curve. As it moves, the gradient of the corresponding tangent will alter continuously, so that the gradient of the curve changes also. For the graph in Figure 1.2(a), the changing behaviour of the gradient can be described as follows.

When x is large and negative (to the left) the curve is falling fast, and so it has a negative gradient of large magnitude. As x becomes smaller in size, but is still negative, the curve flattens out and so the gradient has decreasing magnitude, though it remains negative. Just at $x = 0$, the tangent to the curve is parallel to the x-axis, and so the gradient is zero. As x then increases in the positive direction, the curve begins to rise slowly. It therefore has a small positive gradient. As x grows larger, so the curve rises faster. Its gradient therefore continues to increase, while remaining positive.

This description is a qualititative one. As yet we are not in a position to provide a corresponding *quantitative* description of how the gradient of this curve behaves, beyond noting that it has value zero when $x = 0$. How can actual values be found for the gradient at other values of x?

The gradient of a curved graph at the point A was introduced above as being the gradient of the tangent to the curve at A. Hence, if the equation of this tangent can be found, then the associated gradient of the curve can rapidly be deduced. However, in practice it is no easier to find the equation of the tangent than it is to find the gradient. Indeed, the gradient at a point on a curve is sometimes sought as a preliminary to finding the equation of the tangent! Some other approach is therefore needed in order to find the numerical value of the gradient at any point of a smooth graph.

The verb associated with differentiation is 'to differentiate'. The meaning of this verb in calculus is therefore not the same as its meaning in everyday English (where it means 'to distinguish between' or 'to make different').

This 'other approach' is called *differentiation*, and is the principal mathematical topic of this chapter. Its importance, from the mathematical modelling point of view, lies in the interpretation which can be given to the gradient of a graph in contexts where the graph represents a relationship between two variables.

For the straight lines of Figure 1.1, we may think of the gradient as a measure of *how fast* variable y is changing as variable x changes: a *large* gradient corresponds to a *rapid* change of y with x; a *small* gradient corresponds to a *slow* change of y with x. This allows us to move away from just graphical considerations, since the gradient of the line represents the *rate of change of y with respect to x*.

Similar remarks apply for graphs which are curved, such as the one in Figure 1.2(a), though here the rate of change of y with respect to x, being equal to the gradient at each point, varies as the point moves along the curve. It is differentiation which enables us to find this rate of change at any point. You will see later how this process is carried out.

> In summary, you can think informally of differentiation as a process which enables you to find
>
> ◇   the gradient of a graph at any point on that graph;
>
> ◇   the rate at which one variable changes with respect to another.

Continuous variables

You saw a discussion similar to what follows in Chapter A2, Subsection 7.1.

In the Introduction to Block C, it was mentioned that we were concerned in this block with concepts drawn from continuous rather than from discrete mathematics (as in much of Block B). The following pair of examples should make clear what is meant by 'discrete' and 'continuous', as far as variables are concerned.

The graph in Figure 1.3(a) represents the number of people at a party (including the hostess) against time after 8 pm, which was when the party was scheduled to start. The graph goes up in steps, with gaps between, because it is only possible to have an integer number of party-goers; numbers like 3.5 or 5.9 are simply not possible. A variable, like the number of party-goers here, which can only take on certain distinct values is called a *discrete* variable.

Now look at the graph in Figure 1.3(b), which shows the distance a train has travelled since leaving a station against the time that has elapsed since it started to leave. This distance changes continuously as the train travels along the railway track; it is not constrained to a number of distinct values.

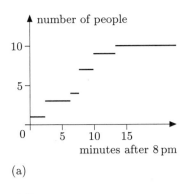

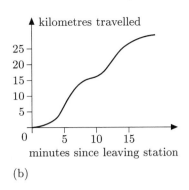

(a)   (b)

Figure 1.3

Distances like 3.5 km or 5.9 km are not only possible but actually occur as the train moves along, as does each number of kilometres between these values. A variable, like distance here, which can change continuously is called a *continuous* variable.

Given the earlier remarks about the need for graphs to be 'locally straight' in order for the gradient of the graph to be found, you may be able to appreciate why differentiation is used only in connection with continuous variables. This should become clearer when a formal description of the differentiation process is reached.

Sometimes a variable which is in fact discrete is modelled as being continuous, because this is adequate for the purposes of the model.

Rates of change

As already stated, the concept of differentiation is linked to rates of change. The idea of rates of change is important, and the four examples which follow should help you to grasp this idea more fully.

Example 1:   Suppose that, when you are on a bus one day, you travel a distance of 300 metres in 30 seconds. Then the bus's average rate of change of distance with respect to time over this period is 300 metres divided by 30 seconds, which is 10 metres per second. In this particular case the rate of change is what we normally call the average *speed* of the bus.

Example 2:   Suppose that the population of a country increases from 50 500 000 to 52 000 000 in 5 years. Then the country's average rate of change of population with respect to time is 52 000 000 − 50 500 000 divided by 5 years, which is 300 000 per year.

Population is actually a discrete variable, but a change of one person in several tens of millions is so tiny, relatively speaking, that the size of a large population can often be regarded conveniently as a continuous variable.

Example 3:   Suppose that the volume of water in a water butt decreases from 300 litres to 100 litres in a 40-minute spell of watering the garden. Then the average rate of change of water volume in the butt with respect to time is 100 − 300 litres divided by 40 minutes, which is −5 litres per minute. Note that this is a negative value because the volume of water is *decreasing* as time increases, whereas the rate of change of population in the previous example was positive, because there the population was *increasing* as time increased.

Example 4:   Finally, suppose that the volume of an inflatable novelty balloon increases from 900 cubic centimetres to 3000 cubic centimetres while the radius increases from 6 centimetres to 9 centimetres. Then the balloon's average rate of change of volume with respect to radius is 3000 − 900 cubic centimetres divided by 9 − 6 centimetres, which is 700 cubic centimetres per centimetre. Note that in this case neither of the variables involved is time.

11

As demonstrated by these examples, _average rates of change_ are found by dividing the increase in one variable by the increase in the other. The phrase 'with respect to' signals that the variable increase which comes afterwards is the one which is to 'do the dividing'.

Dependent and independent variables were first referred to during the audio tape in Chapter B2, Section 1.

As you may remember, the adjectives 'dependent' and 'independent' are used to distinguish between two related variables in such situations. In the first three of the above examples the independent variable is time, and in the last it is the radius. In each case the other variable (distance, population, volume and volume, respectively) is the dependent variable. So we can say that

$$\text{average rate of change} = \frac{\text{increase in dependent variable}}{\text{corresponding increase in independent variable}}.$$

Activity 1.1   Back on the bus

Suppose that, on the next stage of your bus journey mentioned above, the bus travels 1500 metres in 120 seconds, and that on the stage after that it travels 400 metres in 60 seconds. What is its average speed (that is, its average rate of change of distance with respect to time) on each of these stages of the journey?

Comment

Solutions are given on page 79.

Instantaneous rates of change

As Activity 1.1 indicates, it is possible to calculate average rates of change over different stages of a particular activity or process. For the bus journey, you could imagine calculating average rates of change of distance with respect to time (average speeds) over smaller and smaller portions of the journey if you knew enough about the distances and times involved. For instance, if the bus travelled 80 metres during the first 10 seconds of its journey then you would say that its average speed over this portion of the journey was 8 metres per second. A distance of 6 metres travelled between 4 and 5 seconds after the start of the journey corresponds to an average speed over that one-second time interval of 6 metres per second, and so on.

But no matter how short you chose the time intervals to be, the calculation of average rates of change in this way would never provide an exact answer to a question such as 'How fast was the bus going precisely 4 seconds after the start of the journey?'. Notice the different nature of the question here: this is not talking about a rate of change over an interval, known as an _average_ rate of change, but about a rate of change _at a particular instant_ or an _instantaneous_ rate of change.

In the earlier informal summary of what differentiation is, the rate of change referred to should be taken as an instantaneous rather than an average one. Thus instantaneous rates of change are calculated using the process of differentiation.

Note that the word 'instantaneous' is being used here in a specific mathematical way. The _Concise Oxford Dictionary_ gives the everyday meaning of 'instantaneous' as 'occurring or done in an instant or instantly', but it also gives another more specialised interpretation as 'existing at a particular instant'. It is this second meaning which applies here: an instantaneous rate of change exists at a particular instant, that is, at a precise point of time.

Thus an *instantaneous speed* is the speed which an object has at a particular instant. For example, the instantaneous speed of the bus after 4 seconds is the speed which it has when the time is exactly 4 seconds, as measured from the start of its journey.

The instantaneous speed of the bus is in fact the quantity indicated at the time concerned by its speedometer. As the bus's instantaneous speed changes, so the value being indicated by its speedometer varies. At every instant the bus has a corresponding instantaneous speed. This is so even if it is stationary, when the instantaneous speed is zero.

Use of the word 'instantaneous' is natural when the independent variable involved is time. If this is not the case (as in the example above of the expanding balloon, where the independent variable was the radius of the balloon) then the idea of an instant as a 'particular point of time' is replaced by a particular value of the independent variable. We speak then of the rate of change with respect to the independent variable at this particular value, though sometimes the adjective 'instantaneous' is used here also, by analogy with the situation where the independent variable is time.

It is straightforward to calculate average rates of change, and it is possible to obtain estimates for the instantaneous rate of change at any point by finding average rates of change over small intervals which include the selected point, but the process of differentiation is required in order to calculate the exact value of an instantaneous rate of change.

Activity 1.2   *Different meanings*

Some terms introduced in this subsection have been given meanings which differ from their interpretation in everyday English. On Learning File Sheet 2, make a note of these terms and of the meanings which they have been given here. Then try to ensure that you understand these meanings, so that you are not confused by the use of these terms later in the chapter.

As an ongoing activity for the whole chapter, note down other terms you meet which have different meanings from those of everyday English.

Comment

You should have noted at least the following two important terms: to differentiate, instantaneous. You may also have identified others.

1.2 How fast were they jogging?

This subsection is largely given over to an extended example which features the motions of three joggers. You should regard this as an illustration which is purely imaginary. It is unlikely that any real-life joggers would run exactly in the manner described, though perhaps some joggers run in similar ways. In any case, our aim here is to refer to a situation which you should be able to visualise fairly easily, in order to introduce some important points about differentiation. We make the simplifying assumption that the motion of the joggers is smooth, that is, any jerkiness in their movements is to be ignored.

Imagine that Mary, Jenny and Tom are three friends who sometimes meet at the end of a street and jog along it before turning into the park. They have, however, rather different jogging styles. The graph in Figure 1.4 shows how Mary jogs, plotting the distance which she has travelled along the street, s metres, against the time since she started out, t seconds.

The symbol most commonly used for denoting distance is s.

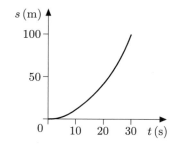

Figure 1.4

The activity below invites you to make some deductions from Figure 1.4.

Activity 1.3   Mary's jogging

(a) How far did Mary jog, according to the graph in Figure 1.4?

(b) How long did she take to jog this distance?

(c) What was her average speed in metres per second (written $\mathrm{m\,s^{-1}}$)?

(d) Did she travel at that speed all along the street? How do you know?

You may not have met the abbreviation $\mathrm{m\,s^{-1}}$ for the units 'metres per second' before. It is equivalent to the older form m/s, but replaces the /s by $\mathrm{s^{-1}}$, much as $1/x$ may be written x^{-1}.

Comment

(a) According to the graph, Mary jogged for 100 metres. This can be read from the vertical axis; the graph starts at $s = 0$ and stops at $s = 100$, and s metres is the distance travelled.

(b) By a similar argument, she took 30 seconds to jog this distance.

(c) Her average speed was 100 metres $\div$ 30 seconds, which is $3.33\,\mathrm{m\,s^{-1}}$, to two decimal places.

(d) No, her speed was variable. You can see this from the shape of the curve. At first it rises quite slowly, but then it becomes steeper. In other words, Mary jogged further in, say, the last ten seconds than in the first ten seconds, which means that her average speed in the last ten seconds was greater than that in the first ten. In fact, her instantaneous speed (as given by the gradient of the tangent to the curve at each time) increased steadily throughout the time that she was jogging.

The answer to the last part of Activity 1.3 reinforces an important idea from Subsection 1.1 that from the *shape* of the graph it is possible to deduce that Mary's speed was not constant, and to describe in qualitative terms the way in which her speed varied.

Activity 1.4 Jenny's and Tom's jogging

(a) Jenny starts jogging at the same time as Mary, and reaches the park (100 metres along the street) when Mary does. She therefore jogs along the street at the same average speed as Mary, but she starts off faster and then progressively slows down. Hence her speed becomes smaller and smaller as she moves along the street. Sketch the graph of Jenny's motion on the axes of Figure 1.5(a).

(b) Tom starts jogging at the same time as Mary and Jenny, and reaches the park when they do, so that he also has the same average speed along the street. However, he jogs steadily, keeping up the same speed all the way to the park. Sketch the graph of Tom's motion on the axes of Figure 1.5(b).

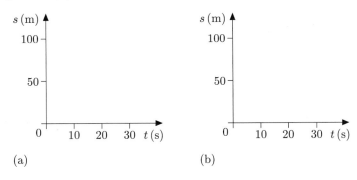

(a)   (b)

Figure 1.5

Comment

(a) Your graph should look something like that in Figure 1.6(a). It should start at the point $(0,0)$ and end at the point $(30, 100)$, and it should rise relatively quickly at first (a higher speed early on) but more slowly later (a lower speed towards the end). Your graph need not be *exactly* the shape shown in Figure 1.6(a), but it should exhibit the features just mentioned.

(b) Your graph should look exactly like that in Figure 1.6(b): a straight line from $(0,0)$ to $(30, 100)$. This is the only way of showing a constant speed.

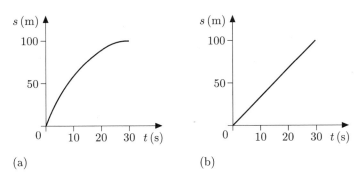

(a)   (b)

Figure 1.6

15

Let's pause and take stock. Each of three joggers takes 30 seconds to jog 100 metres along the same street, so that they all have the same average speed of $3.33\,\mathrm{m\,s^{-1}}$. But they all progress in different ways. Mary starts slowly and then speeds up. Jenny starts faster but then slows down. Tom keeps up a steady pace. All these features can be deduced from the shapes of the graphs of their motion.

While Mary jogged along the street, she had a particular speed at each instant of time. As you saw in Subsection 1.1, this is known as her instantaneous speed. She possessed this speed at each instant even though there was no speedometer to show it (as would have been the case in a vehicle), and its magnitude varied with time.

In fact, the instantaneous speed $v\,\mathrm{m\,s^{-1}}$ is itself a function of time, and because of this it is possible to plot its graph against time for Mary's motion. What shape should this graph have? Clearly the curve should rise with time, because we know that Mary's instantaneous speed increases, but which of the graphs in Figure 1.7 does it resemble most closely?

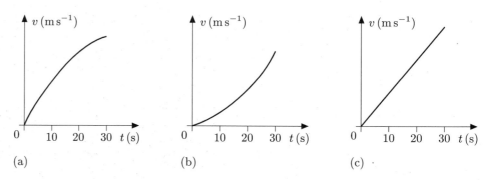

(a)   (b)   (c)

Figure 1.7

We can make progress towards answering this question by looking at Mary's *average* speed over various intervals of time. This could be done by taking appropriate measurements from her distance–time graph (Figure 1.4), but we shall assume here (again for the purposes of illustration) that the relationship between distance and time for Mary's jogging is known to have a particular algebraic form, namely,

Chapter C3 provides guidance on how to choose suitable functions in mathematical models. You may like to confirm that the graph of the equation assumed here has the shape of that in Figure 1.4.

$$s = \frac{t^2}{9} \quad (0 \le t \le 30).$$

Notice the limitations on values of t which appear here. The equation is to be used only between $t = 0$ and $t = 30$, because Mary is running along the street only during this period.

Suppose that we divide up this 30-second period into ten 3-second intervals. We can then find how far Mary ran in each of these intervals, and calculate her average speed over each of them.

Now, on substituting specific values of t into the equation, we see that $s = 0$ when $t = 0$, and that $s = 1$ when $t = 3$. Hence Mary only managed to 'run' 1 metre in the first 3-second interval, with an average speed of $\frac{1}{3}\,\mathrm{m\,s^{-1}}$. Similarly, we have $s = 4$ when $t = 6$. Hence Mary ran $4 - 1 = 3$ metres in the second 3-second interval, at an average speed of $1\,\mathrm{m\,s^{-1}}$. Continuing in this way, we obtain the values shown in the following table.

Table 1.1

Time interval (s)	Average speed $(\mathrm{m\,s^{-1}})$
0–3	$\frac{1}{3}$
3–6	$\frac{3}{3} = 1$
6–9	$\frac{5}{3}$
9–12	$\frac{7}{3}$
12–15	$\frac{9}{3} = 3$
15–18	$\frac{11}{3}$
18–21	$\frac{13}{3}$
21–24	$\frac{15}{3} = 5$
24–27	$\frac{17}{3}$
27–30	$\frac{19}{3}$

Notice that Mary's average speed is increasing by a constant amount from each 3-second interval to the next.

Question: What is this constant amount?

Answer: $\frac{2}{3}\,\mathrm{m\,s^{-1}}$.

Figure 1.8 shows the average speeds of Table 1.1 plotted against time. You can see here the constant increase between one value and the next.

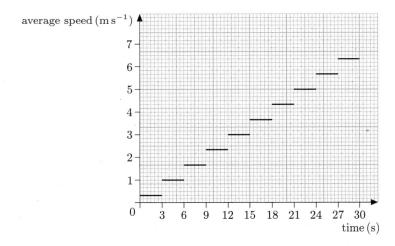

Figure 1.8

Question: Which of the graphs in Figure 1.7 do you now feel is most likely to be appropriate for Mary's instantaneous speed?

Answer: Based on the evidence so far, it looks as if the straight line in Figure 1.7(c) is the most appropriate.

In fact, if we looked in a similar way at Mary's average speed over thirty one-second intervals, then we would again see a constant increase from each interval to the next, suggesting once more that the graph of Figure 1.7(c) is the most appropriate for her instantaneous speed. So it is not altogether surprising that if the process of differentiation is applied to the equation

$$s = \frac{t^2}{9} \quad (0 \le t \le 30),$$

in order to find the instantaneous speed, then the result turns out to be the equation of a straight line. In fact, this equation is

$$v = \frac{2t}{9} \quad (0 \le t \le 30).$$

You will see how to carry out the process of differentiation for yourself later in this chapter. For the moment, just accept this result.

We may also describe this step in terms of functions. Differentiation of the smooth and continuous function $t \longmapsto t^2/9$ (for the distance s) has resulted in the function $t \longmapsto 2t/9$ (for the instantaneous speed v), for all values of t between $t = 0$ and $t = 30$.

The equation

$$v = \frac{2t}{9} \quad (0 \le t \le 30)$$

enables us to find Mary's speed at any instant of time when she was running along the street. For example, her speed ten seconds after starting out (at $t = 10$) is found by substituting $t = 10$ into the equation for v, to produce

$$v = \frac{2 \times 10}{9}$$

$$= 2.22 \quad (\text{to } 2 \, \text{d.p.}),$$

so ten seconds after starting out her instantaneous speed is $2.22 \, \mathrm{m\,s^{-1}}$.

For convenience the words 'decimal places' and 'significant figures' are often abbreviated to d.p. and s.f. respectively.

Activity 1.5   Mary's instantaneous speed

(a) Find Mary's instantaneous speed after she has been running for

   (i) 3 seconds;

   (ii) 20 seconds.

(b) Compare the three instantaneous speeds which you now have with the average speeds tabulated in Table 1.1. Are there any obvious relationships?

Comment

Solutions are given on page 79.

Now consider Jenny's motion. Remember that Jenny starts quickly but then slows down. The rough shape of her distance–time graph is shown in Figure 1.6(a) on page 15. We would expect a graph of her instantaneous speed, $v \, \mathrm{m\,s^{-1}}$, to *fall* as t increases, but once again, we cannot at the outset say anything about the nature of this decrease. Which of the graphs in Figure 1.9 is likely to be the most appropriate in this case?

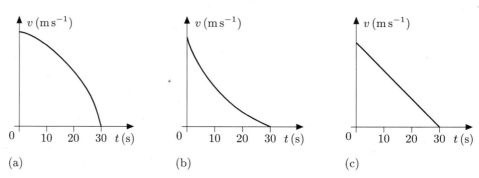

(a)   (b)   (c)

Figure 1.9

We can again deduce the most appropriate shape by looking at average speeds over short time intervals, and again we start by assuming an algebraic description for Jenny's motion, namely

$$s = 100 \sin\left(\frac{\pi t}{60}\right) \quad (0 \le t \le 30),$$

where the argument of the sine function is measured in radians. Here, s metres is the distance Jenny has jogged from the end of the street at time t seconds after starting out.

We can now calculate her average speed over successive 3-second intervals, as was done earlier for Mary. For instance, when $t = 0$ Jenny is at $s = 0$, and when $t = 3$ she is at $s = 100 \sin(\pi/20)$, which equals 15.6434 to four decimal places. So the average speed over this interval is $5.21 \, \text{m s}^{-1}$, to two decimal places.

On repeating this type of calculation for each of the other 3-second intervals in turn, we obtain the values shown below, where the average speeds are given to two decimal places.

Table 1.2

Time interval (s)	Average speed (m s^{-1})
0–3	5.21
3–6	5.09
6–9	4.83
9–12	4.46
12–15	3.98
15–18	3.40
18–21	2.73
21–24	2.00
24–27	1.22
27–30	0.41

Jenny's average speed over these time intervals is decreasing, as expected, but the size of this decrease is not a constant amount from one time interval to the next, as was the case for the increase in Mary's speed. Instead, Jenny's average speed over 3-second intervals falls much more slowly near the start than it does towards the end.

Question: Which of the graphs in Figure 1.9 now looks the most appropriate for Jenny's instantaneous speed?

Answer: The graph in Figure 1.9(a) looks the most appropriate, because it decreases more slowly for smaller values of t than for larger values of t. In this case, if differentiation is applied to the equation

$$s = 100 \sin\left(\frac{\pi t}{60}\right) \quad (0 \le t \le 30),$$

then the result is the equation

$$v = \frac{5\pi}{3} \cos\left(\frac{\pi t}{60}\right) \quad (0 \le t \le 30)$$

for the instantaneous speed, $v \, \text{m s}^{-1}$. This may appear a little forbidding,

This choice of function is *not* the simplest available which fits the shape of graph shown in Figure 1.6(a), and hence would be questionable if viewed purely from the modelling point of view. It is chosen here so that certain mathematical points can be made later in the text.

If you want to check these values, make sure that your calculator is in radian mode. Notice that each intermediate result should be calculated to more decimal places than the final one, as in the text above, to avoid rounding errors.

Again, you will see how to carry out the process of differentiation for yourself later in the chapter.

but its graph certainly has the shape which we were expecting, as you can see from Figure 1.10. Here the average speed values of Table 1.2 and the graph of Jenny's instantaneous speed function have been plotted on the same axes. Notice that differentiation has again led to a function. We started with a smooth, continuous function $t \longmapsto 100\sin(\pi t/60)$, and differentiation then gave a continuous function $t \longmapsto \frac{5}{3}\pi \cos(\pi t/60)$.

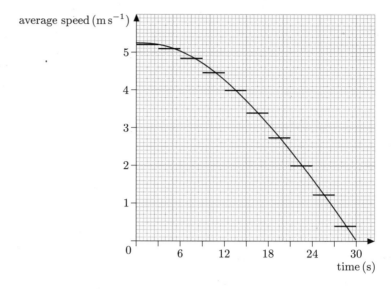

Figure 1.10

If you want to know Jenny's instantaneous speed at any time, then you can find it from the above equation for v. For example, her instantaneous speed after 15 seconds is obtained by substituting $t = 15$ into the equation for v, to give

$$v = \frac{5\pi}{3}\cos\left(\frac{\pi}{4}\right) = 3.70 \quad \text{(to 2 d.p.)}.$$

So her instantaneous speed after 15 seconds is $3.70\,\mathrm{m\,s^{-1}}$.

Now what about Tom? Tom's motion is a special case. Because he ran steadily all the way along the street, his instantaneous speed did not vary: it always equalled his average speed over the 30-second interval. Hence the equation which represents his instantaneous speed does not involve the variable t at all. It is

$$v = \frac{10}{3} \quad (0 \le t \le 30).$$

This is associated with Tom's distance–time graph, which is the straight line of Figure 1.6(b). This straight line has equation

$$s = \frac{10}{3}t \quad (0 \le t \le 30),$$

and differentiation of this gives the constant expression above for v.

The instantaneous speed will always be a constant (and equal to the average speed) when the distance–time graph is a straight line. In all other cases the instantaneous speed varies with time.

The instantaneous speeds of joggers are not of major importance. There are, however, many situations where the knowledge of the instantaneous speed of an object is very important. This new process called differentiation is potentially of great value in these situations involving motion. You will see some such situations later in the chapter.

Before the conclusion of this section, there is a short postscript. In Subsection 1.1 several different rates of change were referred to: of distance with respect to time, of population with respect to time, of volume of water with respect to time and of the volume of a balloon with respect to its radius. In the current subsection we have concentrated so far only on the rate of change of distance with respect to time. This focus should not obscure the fact that the process of differentiation can be used to find other instantaneous rates of change besides those relating to distance and time. This is illustrated briefly in the examples below and by Activity 1.6.

Example 1: Suppose that the equation

$$P = 12\,000\,000 \exp(0.01t) \quad (0 \leq t \leq 10)$$

is used to model how a particular human population of size P varies with time t years in the 10 years after a census. Differentiation then enables us to find the instantaneous rate at which P is changing with respect to t, that is, the rate at which the population changes with respect to time.

Example 2: Suppose that the equation

$$M = -10P^2 + 320P - 2420 \quad (12 \leq P \leq 20)$$

models how a company's profit £M depends upon the price £P at which its (only) product is sold. Differentiation here gives us the instantaneous rate at which M is changing with respect to P, that is, the rate at which the profit changes with respect to the price, for any particular value of that price.

Activity 1.6   Speed from the starting grid

Suppose that the equation

$$v = 5t + t^2 \quad (0 \leq t \leq 2)$$

models how the instantaneous speed $v\,\mathrm{m\,s^{-1}}$ of a racing car depends on the time t seconds after the start of a race. What does differentiation enable us to find in this case?

Comment

A solution is given on page 79.

Summary of Section 1

This section has introduced three important points.

◇   The gradient of a graph at any point on it is defined as being the gradient of the tangent to the graph at that point.

◇   Differentiation may be described informally as a process by which such a gradient can be found. It is also a process which calculates the instantaneous rate of change of a continuous variable y with respect to another continuous variable x.

◇   If the variable y is a linear function of x (that is, the graph is a straight line), then the instantaneous rate of change of y with respect to x is constant and equal to the average rate of change over any interval (the gradient of the line). If the variable y is not a linear function of x, then in general the instantaneous rate of change of y with respect to x does not equal an average rate of change. The instantaneous rate of change of y with respect to x is a function of x.

2 Gradients, tangents and limits

To study this section, you may need a calculator. For Subsection 2.4, you will need to watch Video Band C. However, this video may be watched usefully at any time during your study of the chapter.

2.1 Gradients and tangents

In Subsection 1.1 you saw an informal description of differentiation based on the gradient of a curve and on the related idea of an instantaneous rate of change. Then in Subsection 1.2 we looked at a particular form of rate of change, namely the speed of three imaginary joggers. We now return to the question of how the gradients of curves may be calculated (that is, how the process of differentiation may be carried out) while remaining in the jogging context.

In fact, we shall concentrate on the equation introduced to describe Mary's jogging, which was

$$s = \frac{t^2}{9} \quad (0 \le t \le 30),$$

where s metres is the distance from the start of her run after a time t seconds. It was claimed in Subsection 1.2 that differentiation would give her corresponding instantaneous speed $v\,\mathrm{m\,s}^{-1}$ as

$$v = \frac{2t}{9} \quad (0 \le t \le 30).$$

From this second equation you can find Mary's speed at any instant of time. For example, after 12 seconds her instantaneous speed is

$$\frac{2 \times 12}{9} \,\mathrm{m\,s}^{-1}$$

which is $\frac{8}{3} = 2.67\,\mathrm{m\,s}^{-1}$ to two decimal places.

What would a graphical approach show us? Look at Figure 2.1, which features the graph of the equation

$$s = \frac{t^2}{9} \quad (0 \le t \le 30).$$

The straight line drawn here joins the first and last points on the curve, that is, $(0,0)$ and $(30, 100)$. A line segment which joins any two points on a curve is called a *chord* of the curve, and the gradient of this chord is $\frac{100}{30} = 3.33$ (to two decimal places). That value may look familiar, because you saw in Subsection 1.2 that $3.33\,\mathrm{m\,s}^{-1}$ was Mary's average speed over the whole thirty-second period of her jogging. This is no coincidence, because the gradient of the chord is given by

$$\frac{\text{increase in value of } s}{\text{increase in value of } t},$$

By 'numerical value' here we mean the *number* which describes the speed, without the corresponding units.

which gives the numerical value of

$$\frac{\text{distance travelled}}{\text{time taken}}.$$

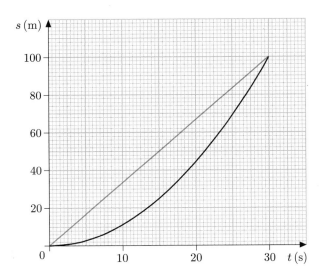

Figure 2.1

Hence the *gradient of the chord* in Figure 2.1 gives the numerical value of the *average speed*.

Now look at Figure 2.2. This again features the graph of the equation $s = t^2/9$ $(0 \leq t \leq 30)$, but now there are three chords superimposed on it:

(a) from $(0,0)$ to $(10, \frac{100}{9})$;

(b) from $(10, \frac{100}{9})$ to $(20, \frac{400}{9})$;

(c) from $(20, \frac{400}{9})$ to $(30, 100)$.

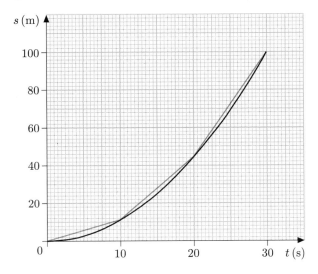

Figure 2.2

Question: What do the gradients of these chords represent?

Answer: The gradient of the chord from $(0,0)$ to $(10, \frac{100}{9})$ gives the numerical value of Mary's average speed for the first ten seconds she was running. Similarly, the gradient of the chord from $(10, \frac{100}{9})$ to $(20, \frac{400}{9})$ gives the numerical value of her average speed over the next ten seconds, and the gradient of the chord from $(20, \frac{400}{9})$ to $(30, 100)$ gives the numerical value of her average speed over the last ten seconds.

This correspondence applies to *any* chord of the curve. The gradient of such a chord will give the numerical value of Mary's average speed over that time interval. In fact, the idea extends even further. An average speed is an average rate of change, and the gradients of chords give average rates of change in general.

The portion of the curve in Figure 2.3 looks fairly straight. Many portions of curves look straight if you zoom in closely enough.

Look next at Figure 2.3, which is once more a graph of the equation $s = t^2/9$, but restricted now to the time interval from $t = 10$ to $t = 14$. This interval is centred on $t = 12$, and above we calculated the *instantaneous* speed at that time to be $\frac{8}{3} = 2.67\,\mathrm{m\,s^{-1}}$ to two decimal places.

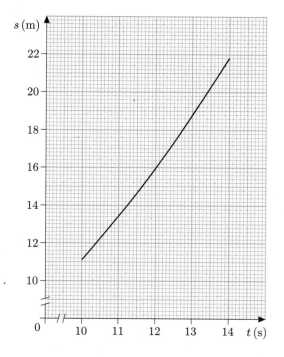

Figure 2.3

The gradient of any chord of this curve is given by

$$\frac{\text{increase in value of } s}{\text{increase in value of } t}.$$

For the chord from $t = 11$ to $t = 12$, the value of s changes from $11^2/9$ when $t = 11$ to $12^2/9$ when $t = 12$, so the gradient is

$$\frac{12^2/9 - 11^2/9}{12 - 11},$$

which works out to $\frac{23}{9}$ or 2.56 to two decimal places. Mary was speeding up as she jogged, so it's not surprising that her average speed in the second leading up to $t = 12$ is a small amount less than her instantaneous speed at $t = 12$.

Similarly, the gradient of the chord from $t = 12$ to $t = 13$ is

$$\frac{13^2/9 - 12^2/9}{13 - 12},$$

which is $\frac{25}{9}$ or 2.78 to two decimal places. Hence, as expected, Mary's average speed in the second following $t = 12$ is a little more than her instantaneous speed at $t = 12$.

Suppose that we take shorter chords, with time intervals whose ends are just 0.1 seconds apart. Then the gradient of the chord from $t = 11.9$ to $t = 12$ is

$$\frac{12^2/9 - 11.9^2/9}{12 - 11.9},$$

which gives 2.66 to two decimal places.

The gradient of the chord from $t = 12$ to $t = 12.1$ is

$$\frac{12.1^2/9 - 12^2/9}{12.1 - 12},$$

which is equal to 2.68, again to two decimal places. Notice how these last two chord gradients are very close to (what we have claimed is) the numerical value of Mary's instantaneous speed at $t = 12$, with one a little smaller and the other a little larger.

This suggests that if shorter and shorter chords near $t = 12$ are taken, the corresponding gradients will be closer and closer to the numerical value of the instantaneous speed at $t = 12$. This conjecture is checked below with a table of values.

Table 2.1

Chord from $t = 12$ to $t =$	Gradient (to 8 d.p.)
13	2.777 777 78
12.1	2.677 777 78
12.01	2.667 777 78
12.001	2.666 777 78
12.0001	2.666 677 78

This process can also be carried out while the chords approach $t = 12$ from below, with the other interval end-point at 11, 11.9, 11.99 etc. The gradient values again converge towards $\frac{8}{3}$, but this time from below.

As you can see, the gradient appears to be approaching closer and closer to exactly $\frac{8}{3}$, the numerical value of the instantaneous speed at $t = 12$. Indeed, this value is the *limit* of the gradient as the length of the chord approaches zero (that is, as the tabulated value of t approaches 12).

We consider next how this can be depicted on a graph. We referred in Subsection 1.1 to the tangent to a curve at a given point A on it, that is, the line through A which just touches the curve at that point, without cutting the curve at another point near A. Figure 2.4 shows the tangent to the curve $s = t^2/9$ $(0 \leq t \leq 30)$ at $t = 12$. If you take any corresponding measurements of 'rise' and 'run' for this line then you should find that, as nearly as you can measure, its gradient is $\frac{8}{3}$. Moreover, this tangent can be identified visually as the 'limit' of the lines for which gradients of chords are considered above, as the chord length approaches zero.

This point about the visual 'limit' may become clearer after you have seen the video for this chapter.

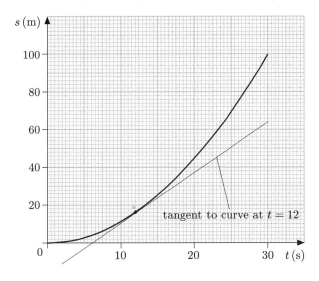

tangent to curve at $t = 12$

Figure 2.4

As mentioned in Subsection 1.1, the gradient of the curve itself at any point is defined to be the gradient of the tangent to the curve at that point, which is also the numerical value of the instantaneous rate of change (here instantaneous speed) at that point. This idea of the gradient of a curve at a point on it is an important one. A straight line has a constant gradient at all points along it, whereas curves have gradients which vary along them, since the gradients of the corresponding tangents vary.

The gradient changes continuously all along the curve

$$s = \frac{t^2}{9} \quad (0 \leq t \leq 30),$$

and so the gradient itself must be a function of t. This function is that for Mary's instantaneous speed $v\,\mathrm{m\,s}^{-1}$, which was quoted earlier as

$$v = \frac{2t}{9} \quad (0 \leq t \leq 30).$$

Since the gradient of a distance–time graph at any point equals the numerical value of the instantaneous speed at that point, this last equation also describes the gradient function. In other words, if g denotes the gradient function for Mary's distance–time graph, then

$$g(t) = \frac{2t}{9} \quad (0 \leq t \leq 30).$$

Differentiation gives a means of finding the gradient function quickly and accurately, provided an algebraic expression for the rule of the original function is known. A graphical alternative is to draw in the tangent to the graph at various points along it by eye, find the gradient of each tangent by making appropriate 'rise' and 'run' measurements, and then plot a graph to show how these gradients vary. This alternative is slow, tedious and error-prone.

We stated earlier that the formula for v was obtained by the process of differentiation. This process (which we have yet to explain in detail) is illustrated effectively by the manner in which the gradient values in Table 2.1 tend to the limit $\frac{8}{3}$. This limit (at the point on the graph for which $t = 12$) is indeed the same as the value which we obtained previously by substituting $t = 12$ into the quoted formula for v, and you will find that the same applies at any other point on the graph which you choose. This indicates how differentiation may be carried out at an individual point, and you will see shortly that the process can be applied to a whole function (that is, for all points on its graph) in a similar way, with the individual point being now an arbitrarily chosen point on the graph. This brief description is expanded upon in the next subsection.

Activity 2.1   Jenny's jogging again

Use a result quoted in Subsection 1.2 to write down the gradient function for the graph whose equation is

$$s = 100 \sin\left(\frac{\pi t}{60}\right) \quad (0 \leq t \leq 30).$$

Comment

A solution is given on page 79.

The context above related to jogging, and so the rate of change involved was speed. However, the mathematical considerations here apply to a pair of related variables and the corresponding rate of change in any situation where the variables are continuous and one of the variables may be expressed algebraically as a function of the other.

2.2 *Limits and derived functions*

We have already referred on several occasions to the process known as *differentiation*, giving an informal description of it and quoting the outcomes of applying this process in a couple of cases. We now adopt a more formal approach to differentiation, including before long a mathematical description of precisely what this process entails.

It was said earlier that differentiation involves finding the gradient of the graph of a given function. For the particular example

$$s = \frac{t^2}{9} \quad (0 \le t \le 30),$$

we claimed that differentiation produces the gradient function

$$g(t) = \frac{2t}{9} \quad (0 \le t \le 30).$$

At $t = 12$, this gave the gradient value as $g(12) = \frac{8}{3}$, and you saw that $\frac{8}{3}$ also appeared to be increasingly close to the values in the right-hand column of Table 2.1 on page 25, which are the gradients of chords to the curve $s = t^2/9$ with left-hand end fixed at $t = 12$ and right-hand end chosen to be closer and closer to $t = 12$. In fact, the chord gradient values in Table 2.1 were obtained by calculating the quotient

$$\frac{(12+h)^2/9 - 12^2/9}{(12+h) - 12}, \quad \text{or equivalently} \quad \frac{(12+h)^2/9 - 12^2/9}{h}, \quad (2.1)$$

for the successive values $h = 1, 0.1, 0.01, 0.001, 0.0001$. Hence our assertion that these gradient values become increasingly close to $\frac{8}{3}$ as the size of h decreases may be interpreted as a claim about the *limiting* value which the quotient (2.1) attains as h tends to zero. We write this claim mathematically as

$$\lim_{h \to 0} \left[\frac{(12+h)^2/9 - 12^2/9}{h} \right] = \frac{8}{3}. \quad (2.2)$$

Here the notation

$$\lim_{h \to 0} [\dots]$$

is pronounced as 'the limit as h tends to zero of …' where … represents the mathematical expression inside the square brackets.

Equation (2.2) is so far a claim which we have made, and which the results in Table 2.1 provide support for, but it is possible to justify its validity by manipulating the quotient (2.1), and you will see next how this is done. The quotient is

$$\frac{(12+h)^2/9 - 12^2/9}{h} = \frac{(12+h)^2 - 12^2}{9h}$$

$$= \frac{144 + 24h + h^2 - 144}{9h}$$

$$= \frac{24h + h^2}{9h}$$

$$= \frac{h(24 + h)}{9h}$$

Assuming that h is not zero (even though it may be very small), the hs here can be cancelled between the numerator and the denominator, giving

$$\frac{24 + h}{9}.$$

From here on we shall drop the condition $0 \le t \le 30$, which related to the specific jogging context considered in Subsection 1.2. Without this condition, the outcome of differentiating $t^2/9$ remains $2t/9$.

The left-hand side of equation (2.2) is therefore equal to

$$\lim_{h \to 0} \left[\frac{24 + h}{9} \right].$$

As h tends to zero, this expression tends to $\frac{24}{9}$, which is $\frac{8}{3}$, verifying that equation (2.2) is indeed valid.

This approach of taking the limit of a quotient works in a similar way if we start from a point other than $t = 12$, with the value of t at that point replacing the 12s in the expressions above. For example, at $t = 20$, the gradient of $s = t^2/9$ is given by

$$\lim_{h \to 0} \left[\frac{(20 + h)^2/9 - 20^2/9}{h} \right].$$

Note that we cannot take the limit of this expression as it stands just by putting $h = 0$, as that would give 0/0 which is undefined. We therefore manipulate the expression first to avoid such an outcome.

This expression can be manipulated and evaluated as in the previous case, and the resulting value for the gradient at $t = 20$ is $\frac{40}{9}$. This is identical to the value obtained by substituting $t = 20$ into the claimed gradient function $g(t) = 2t/9$.

Activity 2.2   Verifying the gradient at t = 20

Verify that

$$\lim_{h \to 0} \left[\frac{(20 + h)^2/9 - 20^2/9}{h} \right] = \frac{40}{9}.$$

Comment

A solution is given on page 79.

What we have done above is to differentiate the expression $t^2/9$ at the two points $t = 12$ and $t = 20$, to find the gradient of the curve $s = t^2/9$ at those points. The two outcomes agreed numerically with our claim that the gradient *function* for this curve is $g(t) = 2t/9$. It is but a relatively small step further to verify our claim concerning the gradient function. This generalisation is achieved by pursuing the same limiting argument once more, but with the variable t itself in place of a particular value of t, such as 12 or 20. Thus the gradient of the curve $s = t^2/9$ at any value of t is given by

$$g(t) = \lim_{h \to 0} \left[\frac{(t + h)^2/9 - t^2/9}{h} \right].$$

The quotient in square brackets is

$$\begin{aligned} \frac{(t + h)^2/9 - t^2/9}{h} &= \frac{(t + h)^2 - t^2}{9h} \\ &= \frac{t^2 + 2th + h^2 - t^2}{9h} \\ &= \frac{2th + h^2}{9h} \\ &= \frac{h(2t + h)}{9h}. \end{aligned}$$

Assuming once more that h is not zero, this is equal to

$$\frac{2t + h}{9},$$

so that the gradient function $g(t)$ is

$$\lim_{h \to 0} \left[\frac{2t+h}{9} \right] = \frac{2t}{9},$$

as claimed previously.

Our development here was in terms of the function $f(t) = t^2/9$. The corresponding gradient function $g(t)$ was obtained by evaluating the expression

$$\lim_{h \to 0} \left[\frac{(t+h)^2/9 - t^2/9}{h} \right],$$

which may be written in terms of f as

$$\lim_{h \to 0} \left[\frac{f(t+h) - f(t)}{h} \right]. \qquad (2.3)$$

This last limit may be applied to *any* smooth function f rather than to just our original choice $f(t) = t^2/9$, and the process of doing this is called *differentiation* of the function f.

For a general function f, the quotient

$$\frac{f(t+h) - f(t)}{h}$$

is the gradient of the chord which joins the points $(t, f(t))$ and $(t+h, f(t+h))$ on the graph of f, as shown in Figure 2.5.

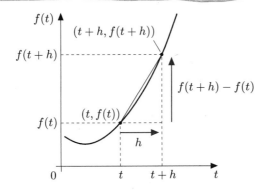

Figure 2.5

Expression (2.3) is the limit of this quotient (gradient) as h tends to zero, that is, the gradient of the tangent to the graph of f at t. If f is a smooth function then this limit can be calculated for any value of t in the domain of the function f, and hence expression (2.3) defines another function, which is called the *derived function* of f and denoted by f'. We also refer to the expression $f'(t)$ as the *derivative* of $f(t)$.

The expressions f' and $f'(t)$ are pronounced respectively as 'f-prime' and 'f-prime of t'.

This terminology should become clearer with further acquaintance, and more is said about the notation involved with differentiation in the following subsection. However, this is an appropriate point at which to highlight the definitions which have just been introduced.

If f is smooth, then this limit is the same whether h takes positive or negative values.

Definitions

◇ If f is a smooth function then the corresponding **derived function** f' is defined by

$$f'(t) = \lim_{h \to 0}\left[\frac{f(t+h) - f(t)}{h}\right], \tag{2.4}$$

where t is any point in the domain of f.

◇ The expression $f'(t)$ (that is, the value of the derived function f' at t) is called the **derivative** of $f(t)$. For a particular value of t, say $t = a$, we refer to $f'(a)$ as the derivative of f (or $f(t)$) at a.

◇ The process of finding the derived function of a function f, or the derivative of $f(t)$, is called **differentiation** of f or $f(t)$. Finding $f'(a)$ is called differentiating f at the point a.

◇ The value of $f'(a)$ gives the gradient of the graph of the function f at a, and the derived function f' is also the gradient function for the graph of f.

We have therefore no further need of the separate symbol g to describe a gradient function.

The terms 'derived function' and 'derivative' are the most general descriptions of the outputs from the process of differentiation. Depending on the particular purpose which you have in differentiating, you may want to regard the derivative as giving the gradient of the original function's graph, or the instantaneous rate of change (which is the speed if the variables involved represent distance and time).

Activity 2.3 The function from Jenny's jogging

In Subsection 1.2, it was claimed that applying differentiation to the equation

$$s = 100\sin\left(\frac{\pi t}{60}\right)$$

results in the equation

$$v = \frac{5\pi}{3}\cos\left(\frac{\pi t}{60}\right).$$

This is equivalent to claiming that if the function f is given by

$$f(t) = 100\sin\left(\frac{\pi t}{60}\right),$$

then the derivative of $f(t)$ is

$$f'(t) = \frac{5\pi}{3}\cos\left(\frac{\pi t}{60}\right).$$

Use equation (2.4) to write down what limiting equality must hold if this claim about the derivative is to be valid.

Comment

A solution is given on page 79.

Activity 2.4   The function from Tom's jogging

In Subsection 1.2, it was claimed that applying differentiation to the equation

$$s = \frac{10}{3}t$$

results in the equation

$$v = \frac{10}{3}.$$

This is equivalent to claiming that if the function f is given by $f(t) = \frac{10}{3}t$, then the derivative of $f(t)$ is $f'(t) = \frac{10}{3}$.

(a) Use equation (2.4) to write down what limiting equality must hold if this claim about the derivative is to be valid.

(b) By finding the limit involved, verify that the derivative of $f(t)$ in this case is as claimed earlier.

Comment

A solution is given on page 80.

In Activity 2.4 you differentiated the function $f(t) = \frac{10}{3}t$, and in the text prior to the definitions above we differentiated the function $f(t) = \frac{1}{9}t^2$. These examples demonstrate how, for simple forms of function, it is possible to apply directly the definition (2.4) of derivative, which is called *differentiating from first principles*. On the other hand, it is much less obvious how to evaluate the limit which you wrote down in Activity 2.3.

It is not usual to differentiate from first principles except in the simplest cases. Beyond these, the common approach is to refer to the known results for certain standard functions (from a table, say) and to rules of differentiation which apply widely. An alternative is to use Mathcad. Beyond this section, you too will be expected to adopt this approach to differentiation, but note that all of the results which we quote later for derivatives can be justified as direct consequences of the definition (2.4).

More attention to some of these justifications is paid in MS221.

Another reason for being aware of this basic definition is that it often appears in mathematical modelling contexts, where the eventual model features a *differential equation*, that is, an equation which involves the derivative of an unknown function. The mathematical argument leading to such an equation may well require the direct application of the limit definition of a derivative, as you will see in later studies.

Activity 2.5   From first principles

Differentiate from first principles, that is, apply equation (2.4) to each of the following functions.

(a) $f(t) = k$,   where k is a constant

(b) $f(t) = t$

(c) $f(t) = t^2$

Comment

Solutions are given on page 80.

2.3 Notations for differentiation

In Subsection 2.2 you saw a formal definition of the derivative of a function $f(t)$, together with the notation $f'(t)$ for this derivative. However, as pointed out in the Introduction to Block C, there is more than one notation in common usage for describing derivatives. While the origin of these differences is partly historical, it is also the case that what the calculus is being studied or used for may determine the most appropriate notation to employ.

The function (prime) notation f' is of more recent introduction than that employed by either Newton or Leibniz. It is the preferred notation of those who study the calculus purely or principally as a branch of mathematics. It arises from the view that functions, rather than variables, are the fundamental objects within the calculus, and that differentiation can be seen as a process which takes one function (f, say) as its input and delivers another function (f') as its output.

Our current mathematical concept of 'function' did not exist during the latter half of the seventeenth century, when calculus was first developed. Newton and Leibniz used ideas more directly related to the geometric problems (finding tangents to curves, for example) with which they were mainly concerned. It was therefore natural for them to think in terms of curves and of variables which are related by the equations of those curves. Indeed, much of the earlier development in this chapter is couched in this form; for example, we referred to the equation

$$s = \frac{t^2}{9} \quad (0 \le t \le 30),$$

connecting the variables s and t, rather than to the function

$$f \colon [0, 30] \longrightarrow \mathbb{R},$$
$$t \longmapsto \frac{t^2}{9}.$$

Newton would have written the derivative in this case by placing a dot above the symbol s, to produce

$$\dot{s} = \frac{2t}{9}.$$

Here $\dot{s}$ (pronounced 's-dot') signifies 'the derivative of s with respect to t'. The 'with respect to t' needs to be said here, because there is no longer explicit mention of the function which relates the two variables. In general, the variable s could also be related to variables other than t, and derivatives (rates of change) with respect to these would differ from the derivative with respect to t.

However, the dot notation applies only when the differentiation is with respect to time, reflecting Newton's principal application of calculus to the study of motion. Thus its conciseness is paid for in not being applicable to describe all rates of change between variables. This notation is still used widely in textbooks relating to motion, especially in physics and engineering, and so you should be able to recognise it and understand what it means.

The notation invented by Leibniz can be used for any pair of related variables, and makes explicit mention of the two variables involved in the differentiation. For the case of

$$s = \frac{t^2}{9},$$

Leibniz would have written the derivative of s with respect to t as

$$\frac{ds}{dt} = \frac{2t}{9}.$$

The expression

$$\frac{ds}{dt}$$

(written ds/dt in running text) is pronounced 'dee-s by dee-t', or sometimes just 'dee-s dee-t'.

As we said, this notation can be applied to differentiation with respect to any variable, not just time. For example, for the equation

$$V = \tfrac{4}{3}\pi r^3,$$

relating the volume V cubic centimetres of a sphere to its radius r centimetres, the derivative of V with respect to r (rate at which volume changes with radius) is written in Leibniz notation as

$$\frac{dV}{dr}$$

(which is pronounced 'dee-V by dee-r').

Leibniz notation places emphasis on the variables rather than on the functions which relate them, and often this is appropriate in modelling contexts. It is used very widely in applied mathematics, science and engineering.

In using this description for a derivative, note that it is a special notation which, despite its appearance, is *not a fraction* in the ordinary sense. In particular, the two ds which appear in it *do not cancel*.

There is a variant of Leibniz notation which is sometimes used. This is to write

Mathcad uses this notation.

$$\frac{ds}{dt} \quad \text{as} \quad \frac{d}{dt}(s),$$

which is pronounced 'dee by dee-t of s'. The assembly of symbols $\frac{d}{dt}$ can be regarded as an instruction to 'differentiate what follows with respect to t'. So if we have

$$s = \frac{t^2}{9},$$

then the derivative of s with respect to t is

$$\frac{d}{dt}(s) = \frac{ds}{dt} = \frac{2t}{9}.$$

This variant has the advantage that explicit mention of the variable s can be avoided altogether if preferred. Thus we may write

$$\frac{d}{dt}\left(\frac{t^2}{9}\right) = \frac{2t}{9},$$

where the left-hand side of the equation is pronounced 'dee by dee-t of t squared over 9'.

Activity 2.6 Saying it out loud

From the learning point of view, it is psychologically important for you to be able to *say* these new notations to yourself or aloud as well as to *read* them. (This ability is of course also necessary in order to communicate orally with others on these matters.) So spend some time saying to yourself:

(a) 'f-prime of t' for $f'(t)$;

(b) 'dee-y by dee-x' for $\dfrac{dy}{dx}$;

(c) 'dee-v by dee-t' for $\dfrac{dv}{dt}$;

(d) 'dee by dee-Q of Q squared' for $\dfrac{d}{dQ} Q^2$;

and so on.

Comment

You should find it much easier to remember and use the various notations if you can also say them. If you feel the need of further practice, then there are numerous examples in the rest of the chapter. You will also be able to practise from here on as you continue with the text.

The various notations can of course be related to one another. For example, if t represents time and y is some time-dependent variable, then the derivative of $y = f(t)$ with respect to t can be denoted in four different but equivalent ways, as

$$\dot{y} = \frac{d}{dt}(y) = \frac{dy}{dt} = f'(t).$$

If variables V and r are related by the equation $V = g(r)$, then the derivative of V with respect to r is

$$\frac{d}{dr}(V) = \frac{dV}{dr} = g'(r).$$

Note however that Leibniz notation has no easy way of writing an expression such as $g'(a)$ for the value of the last derivative at the particular point $r = a$. In Leibniz notation this would be expressed as

$$\left. \frac{dV}{dr} \right|_{r=a}.$$

To conclude this subsection, we discuss briefly why Leibniz adopted a notation for the derivative which 'looks like a quotient' even though, as said above, it is not in fact a normal fraction. Suppose that variables x and y are related by the equation $y = f(x)$, where f is a smooth function. According to our definition (in function notation), the corresponding derivative is

The independent variable t in equation (2.4) has been replaced here by x.

$$f'(x) = \lim_{h \to 0} \left[\frac{f(x+h) - f(x)}{h} \right],$$

which we have said is denoted by dy/dx in Leibniz notation.

The expression in square brackets here is a quotient. Its denominator h is the increase between x and $x + h$. Let us relabel this δx ('a small increase in x').

The numerator is the change between $f(x)$ and $f(x+h)$, which is the corresponding change in the value of y. If we call this δy, then we have

$$\frac{dy}{dx} = \lim_{\delta x \to 0} \frac{\delta y}{\delta x},$$

which indicates why the notation on the left is employed. It is not itself a quotient, but it is the limit of quotients of the form $\delta y / \delta x$ as the denominator δx tends to 0.

The symbol δ is the Greek lower-case letter 'delta'. You should regard δx here as representing a single quantity (small increase in x) and not as $\delta \times x$. A similar remark applies for δy. You may also see such expressions written with the upper-case 'delta', giving Δx and Δy.

2.4   Graphs of derived functions

The video in this subsection concentrates on a visual interpretation of the limiting process at the heart of differentiation, followed by a graphical approach to finding derived functions.

Activity 2.7   The very limit

Watch Video Band C, 'Differentiation'.

Pause, take notes and replay as necessary to ensure that you have grasped the ideas being presented there.

Comment

After watching this video, you should be able to describe in pictorial terms what the process of differentiation involves. You should also have an idea what effect this process has on certain standard functions, including sin, cos, exp and ln. These results are revisited in the next section.

Summary of Section 2

This section introduced the basic definitions and notations associated with differentiation.

◇   If f is a smooth function then the corresponding *derived function* f' is defined by

$$f'(t) = \lim_{h \to 0} \left[\frac{f(t+h) - f(t)}{h} \right], \tag{2.4}$$

where t is any point in the domain of f.

◇   The expression $f'(t)$, that is, the value of the derived function f' at t, is called the *derivative* of $f(t)$. For a particular value of t, say $t = a$, we refer to $f'(a)$ as the derivative of f (or $f(t)$) at a.

◇   The process of finding the derived function of a function f, or the derivative of $f(t)$, is called *differentiation* of f or $f(t)$. Finding $f'(a)$ is called differentiating f at the point a.

◇   The value of $f'(a)$ gives the gradient of the graph of the function f at a, and the derived function f' is the gradient function for the graph of f. If variables x and y are related by the equation $y = f(x)$, then $f'(a)$ is also the instantaneous rate of change of y with respect to x at $x = a$.

◇   There are several notations in current use for derivatives. The function (prime) notation is used above. Newton's notation applies only when the independent variable is time; it consists of putting a dot over the dependent variable (s, say) to indicate its derivative with respect to time as $\dot{s}$. Leibniz notation can be used for any pair of related variables and takes the form dy/dx, where y is the dependent variable and x is the independent variable. This is called the derivative of y with respect to x.

3 Differentiating a variety of functions

To study this section you will need access to your computer, together with the disk with the Mathcad file for this chapter and Computer Book C.

Before the advent of computer algebra packages, mathematicians, scientists and technologists who needed to find the derivatives of functions did so by referring to tables and to lists of rules in textbooks or handbooks (or by memorising some of these). Such tables and rules are still in use, especially where simpler functions are concerned, though computer algebra packages are very helpful for dealing with more complicated functions.

On this course you will be expected to use a table and a couple of rules to find the derivatives of simpler functions, but to rely upon Mathcad in order to differentiate more complicated functions. However, the presence of Mathcad on your computer provides also the opportunity to draw up the table and rules to which you will later refer for simpler functions, and that is part of what you will be doing in the computing activities in this section. Along the way you will also be able to explore, conjecture and test, which should help you to become more comfortable with some of the ideas relating to differentiation.

3.1 Differentiating simpler functions

The main aim in this subsection is to establish (insofar as Mathcad gives these results) the derivatives shown in the table below. For the most part, these should already seem plausible as a result of what you saw on the video in Subsection 2.4.

However, these expressions for the derivatives are obtained by applying Mathcad's symbolic processor. To start with, you will see that its numeric processor can also be of use in differentiation, both to find the derivative of a function at a given point and to draw the graph of a derived function using values at a range of points.

Refer to Computer Book C for the work in this subsection.

In your work during this subsection you obtained the results given in the following table, which is reproduced here for reference.

Table 3.1

Function $f(t)$	Derivative $f'(t)$
1	0
t^n	nt^{n-1}
$\sin t$	$\cos t$
$\cos t$	$-\sin t$
$\exp t$	$\exp t$
$\ln t\ (t > 0)$	$1/t$

The result for t^n holds for any real number n.

An important point to note here is that the results in Table 3.1 for the sine and cosine functions apply only if the variable t is measured in radians.

3.2 Differentiating more complicated functions

In Subsection 3.1 you used Mathcad to draw up a table (shown as Table 3.1) of derivatives for some simple functions. This raises the question of what to do if the function which you need to differentiate does not appear in this table. You could, of course, switch on your computer to perform the new task. However, there are some simple rules which enable you to differentiate a wide range of functions based on those in Table 3.1, and once you are aware of these rules it is probably quicker to apply them than to wait for Mathcad to be ready for use.

In this subsection you will use conjecture-and-test with Mathcad in order to arrive at these rules, before developing some extensions to the results of Table 3.1. We shall then set out clearly the demarcation between those functions which you will be expected to differentiate 'by hand' (including possible reference to a table and rules in the Handbook) and those functions which you will be expected to differentiate only with the help of Mathcad.

You might regard this differentiation as being done 'in your head' rather than 'by hand', especially if you memorise the results which you apply!

Refer to Computer Book C for the work in this subsection.

In your work during this subsection you obtained the derivatives of four simple composite functions. Table 3.2 shows these results, together with two of the derivatives from Table 3.1.

Putting $a = 1$ in Table 3.2 gives the results of Table 3.1.

Table 3.2

Function $f(t)$	Derivative $f'(t)$
1	0
t^n	nt^{n-1}
$\sin(at)$	$a\cos(at)$
$\cos(at)$	$-a\sin(at)$
$\exp(at)$	$a\exp(at)$
$\ln(at)\ (at > 0)$	$1/t$

You also saw how the derivatives of sums, differences and constant multiples of functions can be deduced from the following rules.

Constant multiple and sum rules

◇   The **Constant Multiple Rule** states that, if f is a smooth function and c is a constant, then the derivative of $cf(t)$ is

$$\frac{d}{dt}(cf(t)) = cf'(t),$$

where $f'(t)$ is the derivative of $f(t)$.

◇   The **Sum Rule** states that, if f and g are smooth functions, then the derivative of the sum $f(t) + g(t)$ is

$$\frac{d}{dt}(f(t) + g(t)) = f'(t) + g'(t),$$

where $f'(t)$ is the derivative of $f(t)$ and $g'(t)$ is the derivative of $g(t)$.

◇   Likewise, the derivative of the difference $f(t) - g(t)$ is

$$\frac{d}{dt}(f(t) - g(t)) = f'(t) - g'(t).$$

This difference is the sum of $f(t)$ and $-1 \times g(t)$, so the result follows from those for the Constant Multiple and Sum Rules.

The next box specifies which functions you are expected to differentiate in this course without the aid of Mathcad.

In particular, you may be expected to carry out such differentiations in the examination.

Differentiating 'by hand'

You will be expected to differentiate 'by hand' any of the following:

◇   a function of any of the forms shown in the left-hand column of Table 3.2 ;

◇   any constant multiple of such a function;

◇   any sum or difference of such functions;

◇   any sum or difference of constant multiples of such functions.

For any other type of function, you will be expected to find the derivative only by using Mathcad.

Summary of Section 3

This section was concerned with drawing up a table and establishing some rules to help with differentiation.

◇   The derivatives of some commonly-occurring functions appear in Table 3.2 on page 38.

◇   The *Constant Multiple Rule* states that, if f is a smooth function and c is a constant, then the derivative of $cf(t)$ is

$$\frac{d}{dt}(cf(t)) = cf'(t),$$

where $f'(t)$ is the derivative of $f(t)$.

◇   The *Sum Rule* states that, if f and g are smooth functions, then the derivative of the sum $f(t) + g(t)$ is

$$\frac{d}{dt}(f(t) + g(t)) = f'(t) + g'(t),$$

where $f'(t)$ is the derivative of $f(t)$ and $g'(t)$ is the derivative of $g(t)$.

Also, the derivative of the difference $f(t) - g(t)$ is

$$\frac{d}{dt}(f(t) - g(t)) = f'(t) - g'(t).$$

◇   In this course you will be expected to differentiate without using Mathcad any function of one of the forms shown in Table 3.2, which is repeated in the course Handbook. You will also be expected to be able to apply the Constant Multiple and Sum Rules where appropriate. Mathcad can be used to differentiate more complicated functions.

Exercises for Section 3

Exercise 3.1

Differentiate each of the following functions, without using Mathcad.

(a) $f(t) = t^2 \sqrt{t} \quad (t > 0)$

(b) $f(y) = \dfrac{1}{y^3} + \cos(5y) \quad (y > 0)$

(c) $f(s) = 14 \sin\left(\dfrac{s}{7}\right)$

(d) $f(x) = 3(\exp(5x) - \exp(-5x))$

(e) $f(v) = 2 \ln\left(\dfrac{v}{8}\right) \quad (v > 0)$

Exercise 3.2

Differentiate the following functions, without using Mathcad. In each case you will need to express the function in a different but equivalent form, before the results of this section may be applied.

(a) $f(t) = (t - 1)^3$

(b) $f(z) = \exp(1 + 2z)$

(c) $f(y) = \ln(y^3) \quad (y > 0)$

(d) $f(x) = \sin(1 + x)$

> *Hint:*   Here you will need to apply the trigonometric identity
>
> $$\sin(\alpha + \beta) = \sin \alpha \cos \beta + \cos \alpha \sin \beta,$$
>
> which you may have encountered in earlier study. The derivative which results can be rewritten using the second identity
>
> $$\cos(\alpha + \beta) = \cos \alpha \cos \beta - \sin \alpha \sin \beta.)$$

4 Modelling motion using differentiation

You will need a calculator in order to study this section.

In the latter part of Section 2 and in Section 3 you were asked to consider differentiation purely as a mathematical process. In this section and in Section 5 the emphasis returns to the starting point of this chapter, that is, ways in which differentiation can be applied to the analysis and solution of practical problems.

In Subsection 2.3 you were introduced to the variety of notation which is used to describe derivatives. In Section 3 the focus was on differentiating a function $f(t)$, so that an appropriate notation for the derivative was $f'(t)$ or, where Mathcad was directly involved,

$$\frac{d}{dt} f(t).$$

In applications, the direct focus is usually upon a pair of related variables rather than on just the function which relates them, and it is therefore most convenient to use the (original form of) Leibniz notation to describe derivatives, since this includes mention of the two variables concerned. For example, in the jogging illustration introduced in Subsection 1.2, the equation for Mary's jogging was

$$s = \frac{t^2}{9} \quad (0 \le t \le 30),$$

where s metres was her distance from the starting point at t seconds after she started out. The derivative of s with respect to t is denoted in Leibniz notation by ds/dt. You saw the derivative for this particular case obtained from first principles in Subsection 2.2. In Leibniz notation it is expressed as

$$\frac{ds}{dt} = \frac{2t}{9} \quad (0 \le t \le 30).$$

Notice the way in which the variables s and t appear in the left-hand side of this equation: the *dependent* variable is placed above and the *independent* variable is below. This agrees with what was said about average rates of change in Subsection 1.1.

In the rest of this chapter we shall use differentiation in situations like this where there are two variables involved, and Leibniz notation will be used in the manner just described.

Question: Later in the chapter you will meet variables M and P which are related by the equation

$$M = -10P^2 + 320P - 2420 \quad (12 \le P \le 20).$$

When this equation is differentiated with respect to P, will the resulting left-hand side be written as dM/dP or as dP/dM?

Answer: It will be written as dM/dP, because P appears after 'with respect to', that is, P is the independent variable here.

4.1 The joggers revisited

The example of the three joggers was introduced in Subsection 1.2, before you had seen the formal definition of the derivative (Subsection 2.2) or how to find the derivatives of a wide variety of functions (Section 3). The results given for the distance s m and speed v m s^{-1} of each jogger at time t s after they started (for $0 \le t \le 30$) were as follows.

For Mary: $s = \dfrac{t^2}{9}$ and $v = \dfrac{2t}{9}$.

For Jenny: $s = 100 \sin\left(\dfrac{\pi t}{60}\right)$ and $v = \dfrac{5\pi}{3} \cos\left(\dfrac{\pi t}{60}\right)$.

For Tom: $s = \dfrac{10t}{3}$ and $v = \dfrac{10}{3}$.

It was claimed that the expression for v could be obtained from that for s in each case by differentiation. This was justified directly for Tom, whose instantaneous speed equals his average speed. For Mary (and again for Tom), the derivative was found from first principles in Subsection 2.2.

In the Activity below, you are asked to show that these expressions quoted for the speed v are consistent with the results developed in Section 3.

Activity 4.1   From table and rule

By using Table 3.2 (on page 38) and the Constant Multiple Rule, confirm that differentiation gives the following.

(a) If $s = \dfrac{t^2}{9}$, then $\dfrac{ds}{dt} = \dfrac{2t}{9}$.

(b) If $s = 100 \sin\left(\dfrac{\pi t}{60}\right)$, then $\dfrac{ds}{dt} = \dfrac{5\pi}{3} \cos\left(\dfrac{\pi t}{60}\right)$.

(c) If $s = \dfrac{10t}{3}$, then $\dfrac{ds}{dt} = \dfrac{10}{3}$.

Comment

Solutions are given on page 80.

Your answers to Activity 4.1 confirm that the derivatives which you were asked to take on trust in Subsection 1.2 are indeed consistent with the table of derivatives and the rules which you drew up in Section 3.

So far, we have used the term 'speed' to describe how fast the joggers were moving. There is another term which is commonly used to describe how fast something moves, namely, *velocity*. In everyday English the two words 'speed' and 'velocity' mean much the same, but in mathematics, science and technology there is a significant difference in meaning between them, which is as follows.

A more precise definition of 'velocity' and 'speed' will be given later in this section.

Speed and velocity

◇   The *speed* of an object is a measure of how fast it is moving, irrespective of its direction of motion.

◇   The *velocity* of an object is a measure of how fast it is moving *and* of its direction of motion.

Very often in situations involving motion, the direction of the motion is just as important as the speed. For example, an aeroplane with a velocity of 600 kilometres per hour due north moves very differently from one with a velocity of 600 kilometres per hour due east. For this reason velocities rather than speeds are often used in describing motion.

In this chapter we shall refer principally to velocities from now on, but the examples will be confined to motion along straight lines. In other words, we look here only at *one-dimensional* motions. Let us start by seeing what alters if we describe the motion of the three joggers in terms of velocities instead of speeds, assuming that the street along which they jog is straight.

> If the street were not straight then Tom's *velocity* could not be constant (even though his speed was) because his *direction* of movement would change as he ran along the street.

There is a simple way of indicating the velocity (that is, both the speed and direction) of an object, such as each jogger, moving along a straight line. There are only two possible directions of motion for the object, one being the opposite of the other, so it is reasonable to designate motion in one direction as positive and motion in the opposite direction as negative.

In the case of the joggers, suppose that we take the direction *from* the end of the street where they meet *to* the park as being the positive direction. Then, as they jog towards the park, their velocities $v\,\text{m s}^{-1}$ for $0 \le t \le 30$ will all be positive:

$$\text{for Mary: } v = \frac{2t}{9}; \quad \text{for Jenny: } v = \frac{5\pi}{3}\cos\left(\frac{\pi t}{60}\right); \quad \text{for Tom: } v = \frac{10}{3}.$$

On the other hand, if we choose the positive direction as being *from* the park *to* the end of the street where the joggers meet, then their velocities $v\,\text{m s}^{-1}$ for $0 \le t \le 30$ will all be negative.

If there is freedom to choose the positive direction in describing a one-dimensional motion, then it simplifies matters to choose this direction so as to avoid too many minus signs. The speed for such a motion is just the magnitude (size) of the velocity v, that is, $|v|$.

> The modulus notation, $|x|$, was introduced in Chapter B2 Section 5.

We have described above the difference in meaning between 'speed' and 'velocity'. A similar distinction can be made for the two terms *distance* and *displacement*, for static or moving objects.

Definitions

◇ The **distance** of an object from a fixed point is the measure of how far it is from the fixed point, irrespective of direction.

◇ The **displacement** of an object from a fixed point is the measure of how far it is from the fixed point *and* of its direction relative to that point.

> The word *position* is sometimes used as an alternative to 'displacement'. We say that displacement and velocity are *vector* quantities (having an associated magnitude and direction), whereas distance and speed are *scalar* quantities (having magnitude only).

Notice that in each case it is necessary to have specified a fixed point from which the measurements can be made. This is usually referred to as the *origin* for the measurements. As with velocity, we are interested here in the description of displacements only for objects moving along a straight line, and once again there is a simple way of indicating the direction of such a displacement relative to the origin. Displacement in one direction along the line from the origin is taken to be positive, and then displacement in the opposite direction from the origin is negative. In either case, if s is the displacement of the object, then its distance from the origin is the magnitude of s, that is, $|s|$.

For consistency, the direction from the origin which is chosen as positive for displacements is also taken to be the positive direction for velocity measurements. This ensures that any increase in the numerical value of the displacement corresponds to a positive velocity. Indeed, if s is the displacement of an object and v is its velocity (both dependent on time t), then we have

$$v = \frac{ds}{dt}.$$

Activity 4.2 Jogging forth and back

Suppose that one day Tom arrives early for the jogging session. Rather than standing around while waiting for his friends, he jogs on his own from the usual meeting point (marked M on Figure 4.1 below) to the park entrance (P on Figure 4.1) and back again. As usual he jogs at a steady speed of $\frac{10}{3}\,\mathrm{m\,s^{-1}}$.

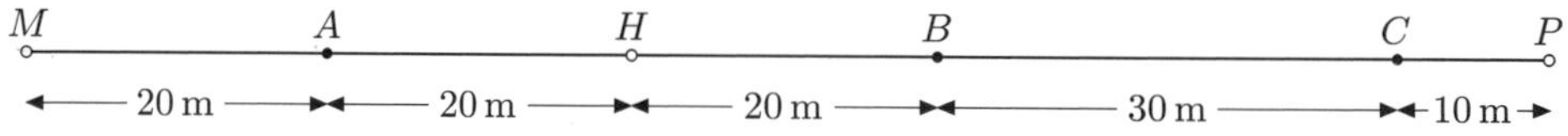

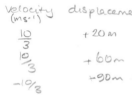

M   A   H   B   C   P

←— 20 m —►◄— 20 m —►◄— 20 m —►◄— 30 m —►◄—10 m—►

Figure 4.1

(a) Let M be the fixed point (origin) for displacement measurements, and take the direction from M to P as positive. Specify Tom's displacement and velocity at each of the points (shown on Figure 4.1)

    (i) A, when he is jogging from M towards P;

    (ii) B, when he is jogging from M towards P;

    (iii) C, when he is jogging from P towards M.

(b) Now suppose that your house (H on Figure 4.1) is taken as the origin for displacement measurements, with the same choice of positive direction as before. What are Tom's displacement and velocity for each of parts (a)(i), (ii) and (iii) in terms of this origin and direction?

Comment

Solutions are given on page 80.

Activity 4.3 More different meanings

You have just met some further terms whose meaning in mathematics, science and technology is a little different from their everyday meaning. We suggested in Activity 1.2 that it would be useful to make a note on Learning File Sheet 2 of such terms as you encounter them. This is therefore an appropriate time to bring your records up to date. Also pause and ensure that you are clear about the meanings of these terms.

Comment

You should have noted the distinction between the meanings of speed and velocity, and that between distance and displacement (or position).

4.2 Acceleration

It was pointed out above that, if s is the displacement of an object in one-dimensional motion and v is its velocity (both dependent on time t), then we have

$$v = \frac{ds}{dt}.$$

In words, the velocity is the (instantaneous) rate of change of displacement with respect to time. This may be regarded as a more precise version of our earlier definition of *velocity*; the derivative ds/dt is, for the motion of an object in a straight line, just what we described earlier as 'the measure of how fast it is moving and of its direction of motion'. As pointed out before, the *speed* of the object is the magnitude $|v|$ of its velocity.

Since the velocity v is time-dependent, we can in turn consider the rate of change of velocity with respect to time, dv/dt. This physical quantity is called the *acceleration* of the object. Denoting acceleration by a, we may write

$$a = \frac{dv}{dt}.$$

In general, the acceleration will again be a function of time. Like displacement and velocity, the acceleration may be positive or negative (or zero). If the velocity increases then the acceleration is positive, but if the velocity decreases then the acceleration is negative. In either case, the acceleration is a measure of how rapidly the velocity is changing.

Definitions

An object in one-dimensional motion has a displacement s which depends upon time t, where s is measured with respect to a particular choice of origin and positive direction along the line of motion.

◇   The **velocity** v of the object is given by

$$v = \frac{ds}{dt}.$$

(instantaneous velocity /acceleration)

◇   The **acceleration** a of the object is given by

$$a = \frac{dv}{dt}.$$

The definitions above are for *instantaneous* velocity ($v = ds/dt$) and *instantaneous* acceleration ($a = dv/dt$). It is also possible to refer to an *average* velocity or acceleration over some time interval. The average velocity is the average rate of change of displacement with respect to time over the interval, and the average acceleration is the average rate of change of velocity with respect to time over the interval.

For example, if a train accelerates along a straight track from rest (the term *rest* is used to indicate zero velocity) to a velocity of $15\,\mathrm{m\,s^{-1}}$ in a time $20\,\mathrm{s}$, then its average acceleration over that interval is 15 metres per second divided by 20 seconds, which is 0.75 metres per second per second. The usual notation for the acceleration unit 'metres per second per second' is $\mathrm{m\,s^{-2}}$, so the average acceleration of the train is $0.75\,\mathrm{m\,s^{-2}}$.

This does not necessarily mean that the instantaneous acceleration is $0.75\,\mathrm{m\,s^{-2}}$ throughout the 20 seconds. The velocity–time graph in Figure 4.2(a) shows a situation where the instantaneous acceleration would be $0.75\,\mathrm{m\,s^{-2}}$ throughout; Figure 4.2(b) shows a situation where it would not. Just as the gradient of a displacement–time graph indicates the instantaneous velocity, so the gradient of a velocity–time graph indicates the instantaneous acceleration. The gradient is constant for the straight-line graph of Figure 4.2(a), with value 0.75. For the graph of Figure 4.2(b), the gradient (which is the instantaneous acceleration) is larger than 0.75 in the early stages of the motion, but then decreases steadily.

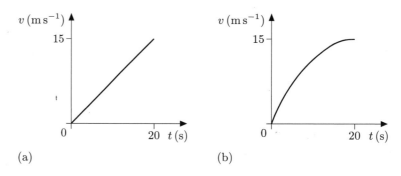

(a) (b)

Figure 4.2

Just as with displacement and velocity, the direction of an acceleration for an object in one-dimensional motion is indicated by its sign. The positive direction for acceleration is the same as that for velocity, that is, the direction of increasing displacement. However, an acceleration can be positive even when motion is in the negative direction (that is, when the velocity is negative) or vice versa.

Example 4.1 Positive and negative acceleration

Consider the following four motions of an object along a straight line, each described by its velocity v as a function of time t for the interval $0 \leq t \leq 10$. In each case, draw the corresponding velocity–time graph, write down the acceleration and describe the motion in words.

(a) $v = t$ (b) $v = 10 - t$ (c) $v = -t$ (d) $v = t - 10$

Solution

The velocity–time graphs for the four cases appear in Figure 4.3 below.

(a) The velocity is $v = t$, so the acceleration is $a = dv/dt = 1$. The object starts from rest, then moves in the positive direction and speeds up steadily.

In saying that the object 'speeds up', we mean that its speed $|v|$ is increasing. Likewise, we say that it 'slows down' when its speed is decreasing.

(b) The velocity is $v = 10 - t$, so the acceleration is $a = dv/dt = -1$. The object moves in the positive direction but slows down steadily, reaching rest at $t = 10$.

(c) The velocity is $v = -t$, so the acceleration is $a = dv/dt = -1$. The object starts from rest but then moves in the negative direction. It speeds up steadily as it continues in this direction.

(d) The velocity is $v = t - 10$, so the acceleration is $a = dv/dt = 1$. The object moves in the negative direction but slows down steadily, reaching rest at $t = 10$.

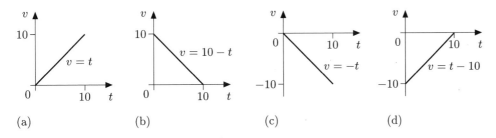

(a)   (b)   (c)   (d)

Figure 4.3

We have given above a precise mathematical definition of what is meant by 'acceleration'. As Example 4.1 may have shown you, this meaning does not always match what would be understood by 'acceleration' in everyday usage. The normal use of 'acceleration' would refer to the magnitude $|a|$ rather than to $a = dv/dt$ itself, and then only in cases where the object is speeding up (as in parts (a) and (c) of Example 4.1). When the object is slowing down (as in parts (b) and (d) of Example 4.1), the value of $|a|$ would normally be referred to as a *deceleration*.

Unlike the situation with displacement and velocity (whose magnitudes are described by the respective terms distance and speed) there is no separate technical word to describe the magnitude $|a|$ of an acceleration.

Example 4.2   Safe landing

A model of the motion of a particular parachutist after the parachute opens leads to the equation

$$v = 8 + 22\exp(-1.25t) \quad (t \geq 0),$$

where $v\,\mathrm{m\,s^{-1}}$ is the instantaneous velocity (taken to be positive in the direction vertically downwards) at time t s after the parachute opens, until such time as the parachutist reaches the ground.

(a) What is the velocity of the parachutist at the moment the parachute is opened, and what is the later terminal velocity (velocity for large values of t)?

(b) Find an expression for a in terms of t, where $a\,\mathrm{m\,s^{-2}}$ is the instantaneous acceleration of the parachutist.

Solution

(a) The parachute opens at time $t = 0$, when the velocity (in $\mathrm{m\,s^{-1}}$) is

$$v = 8 + 22\exp(0) = 8 + 22e^0 = 30.$$

> Recall that $\exp(x)$ is another way of writing e^x.

For large values of t, the expression $\exp(-1.25t)$ tends to zero. Hence the terminal velocity is $v = 8\,\mathrm{m\,s^{-1}}$.

(b) To find the acceleration, we need to differentiate the expression for v. Using the Sum Rule, the Constant Multiple Rule and Table 3.2 (on page 38), we have

$$a = \frac{dv}{dt}$$
$$= 8 \times 0 + 22 \times (-1.25)\exp(-1.25t)$$
$$= -27.5\exp(-1.25t) \quad (t \geq 0),$$

47

and this is the required expression for a. As expected, this acceleration is negative. The velocity is positive (measured downwards) and the parachute is fulfilling its purpose by reducing that velocity from its relatively large initial value down to a terminal value for which injury should be avoided when the parachutist hits the ground.

Activity 4.4   Acceleration of the joggers

Consider once more the three joggers of Subsection 1.2, and take the positive direction for their motion along the straight street as being from their meeting point towards the park. Their velocities $v\,\mathrm{m\,s^{-1}}$ are then as follows, for $0 \le t \le 30$.

(a) For Mary: $v = \dfrac{2t}{9}$

(b) For Jenny: $v = \dfrac{5\pi}{3}\cos\left(\dfrac{\pi t}{60}\right)$

(c) For Tom: $v = \dfrac{10}{3}$

In each case, find an equation for a, where $a\,\mathrm{m\,s^{-2}}$ is their instantaneous acceleration.

Comment

Solutions are given on page 81.

From what has been said so far, you may have realised that you could find the instantaneous acceleration from an expression for the displacement s by differentiating *twice* with respect to t. This follows because we have defined the velocity v to be ds/dt, and the acceleration a to be dv/dt.

For instance, in the case of Mary's jogging, the equation describing the displacement is (taking the fixed point at the end of the street where the joggers meet, and the positive direction as in Activity 4.4)

$$s = \frac{t^2}{9} \quad (0 \le t \le 30).$$

Differentiating this once gives the instantaneous velocity, as

$$v = \frac{ds}{dt} = \frac{2t}{9} \quad (0 \le t \le 30),$$

and differentiating again gives the instantaneous acceleration

$$a = \frac{dv}{dt} = \frac{d^2 s}{dt^2} = \frac{2}{9} \quad (0 \le t \le 30).$$

The last line includes a new piece of notation,

$$\frac{d^2 s}{dt^2}.$$

This is read 'dee-two-s by dee-t-squared', and denotes the **second derivative** of s with respect to t. The second derivative is the result of differentiating twice. Hence ds/dt denotes the derivative (or, if it is necessary to be very precise, the *first* derivative), obtained by differentiating once, and d^2s/dt^2 is the *second* derivative, obtained by differentiating a second time. In other words, we have

$$\frac{d^2s}{dt^2} = \frac{d}{dt}\left(\frac{ds}{dt}\right).$$

This can also be written as

$$\frac{d^2}{dt^2}(s) = \frac{d}{dt}\left(\frac{d}{dt}(s)\right).$$

Mathcad has a d^n/dx^n operator, which can be used to obtain second derivatives with $n = 2$.

In Newton's notation, where the first derivative of s with respect to time is denoted by one dot, as $\dot{s}$, the corresponding second derivative is denoted by two dots, as $\ddot{s}$.

In the function notation, where the first derivative of $f(t)$ is denoted with one prime, as $f'(t)$, the second derivative is denoted with two primes, as $f''(t)$.

So $f'' = (f')'$ denotes the *second derived function* of f (the derived function of the derived function of f).

Activity 4.5   Second derivatives

(a) Find the second derivative of each of the following with respect to the independent variable, and write it using Leibniz notation.

   (i) $s = 8t - 2t^2 \quad (0 \le t \le 2)$

   (ii) $y = 30\exp(0.1x)$

(b) Find the second derivative of the following with respect to t (time), and write it using Newton's notation.

$$x = 2\sin(3t) + 3\cos(3t)$$

Comment

Solutions are given on page 81.

4.3   Modelling the motion of falling objects

The motion of falling objects is of interest in various situations. For instance, those planning parachute jumps need to be certain that landings will be safe. Those responsible for the new leisure pursuit of the early 1990s called bungee-jumping had to ensure that the jumper would be pulled up by the bungee (elastic rope) before hitting the ground. Stunt people need to make sure that the jumps and falls which they carry out in films are reasonably free from the risks of injury, and so on. In many cases trial and error, together with past experience, are used to determine what is safe, but mathematical modelling can be used to help.

In this subsection, we restrict attention to the case of an object falling *vertically*, which is a particular case of motion in a straight line. For such a motion, there is a useful standard model which can be used.

Standard model for falling objects

Under certain circumstances, the displacement s metres of an object falling vertically can be described by the equation

$$s = \tfrac{1}{2}gt^2,$$

where g (in $\mathrm{m\,s^{-2}}$) is the constant *acceleration due to gravity* and t seconds is the time since the object started to fall. Here the origin for displacement measurements is chosen as the starting point of the object's motion (where it is at time $t = 0$), and the positive direction is chosen downwards.

The circumstances in which this equation applies are as follows.

◇   The object starts from rest. In other words, it has zero velocity at time $t = 0$; it is dropped rather than thrown.

◇   There are no forces other than gravity acting on the object. In particular, the effects of air resistance can be ignored.

◇   The object is not spinning.

◇   The fall takes place in calm, wind-free conditions.

If this restriction surprises you, think of how spin can affect the flight of a tennis or cricket ball.

The acceleration due to gravity is an example of a *physical constant*. It is convenient to denote such constants by universally agreed letters, and g is the letter chosen to denote the acceleration due to gravity. In fact its value varies slightly over the surface of the Earth, but is $9.8\,\mathrm{m\,s^{-2}}$ to one decimal place.

The variation in the value of g at sea level is from $9.78\,\mathrm{m\,s^{-2}}$ near the equator to $9.83\,\mathrm{m\,s^{-2}}$ near the North or South Pole.

Note that the equation $s = \tfrac{1}{2}gt^2$ cannot apply to the motion of the parachutist in Example 4.2, because when the parachute is open there is considerable air resistance (in fact, parachutes are designed to rely upon this air resistance). Nor does this model apply to the motion of a bungee-jumper *after* the bungee has become taut, since the bungee then provides an upward pull on the jumper to counteract that of gravity downwards. However, it could be applied to such a jump in the period *before* the bungee becomes taut. In short, the model is valid only for objects in free fall under gravity.

As with the example of the three joggers, this is not intended to be a realistic example, and should be regarded as purely imaginary.

To illustrate how this model can be applied, consider how the motion of a falling rock can be described. Suppose that the rock is to be dropped off the edge of a 35-metre overhanging cliff by the villain in one sequence of a thriller film. The car carrying the heroine of the film is to pass beneath the cliff just as this is happening, and there is to be a near miss. The producer of the film wants to know two things.

◇   How long will the rock take to fall the 35 metres from the cliff edge to the ground?

◇   How fast will the rock be travelling when it hits the ground?

We turn now to the five-stage diagram of the mathematical modelling cycle which was introduced in Chapter A2 Subsection 7.2. This is reproduced as Figure 4.4 below.

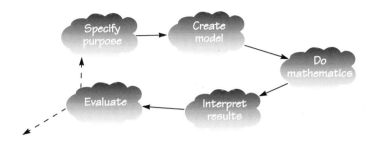

Figure 4.4

According to this diagram, the first modelling stage is to specify the purpose of the model. From the description above, it is clear that the purpose in this case is:

◇   to find out how long the rock takes to fall 35 metres, and how fast it is then travelling.

In order to apply the standard model quoted above, we shall make some appropriate simplifying assumptions about the motion of the rock. This is not so much creating a model (Stage 2 of the modelling cycle), but arranging matters so that an existing model can be used. However, recognising circumstances in which an existing model can be applied is also an important modelling skill.

The assumptions we make are as follows.

◇   The rock starts its fall from rest, and descends vertically.

◇   The effects of air resistance can be ignored. (For a heavy object like a rock falling for a shortish distance, this is not too drastic a simplification.)

◇   The rock is not spinning. (This could be significant, because the easiest way of moving a heavy rock over the edge of a cliff is to roll it off, which means that the rock *will* be spinning. However, this is again unlikely to have a major effect over the distance involved.) In fact the rock is treated as if it is a point at which the mass is concentrated

◇   The conditions are calm and wind-free. (This can be arranged by choosing a suitable day to do the filming, unless the film script stipulates otherwise. Even without these conditions, the motion is unlikely to alter much.)

Notice how these assumptions all relate to the circumstances under which the standard model can be used.

With these assumptions, we are ready to continue with Stage 2 by formulating the mathematical problem. The rock starts from the top of the cliff, and so this is taken as the origin for displacement measurements, with the positive direction chosen downwards.

The relevant variables are the displacement of the stone, s metres from the top of the cliff, and the time since it started falling, t seconds.

The standard model, featuring the equation

$$s = 4.9t^2,$$

then applies. Here we have written 4.9 instead of $\frac{1}{2}g$. The above equation is not, however, valid for all values of t. It only holds while the rock is falling, so that one limitation is $t \geq 0$. There is also an upper bound on t, which is the time at which the rock reaches the ground, but for the moment this largest value of t is unknown (it is actually one of the pieces of information which the model has been set up to find). On the other hand, we do know that s must be no more than 35, because the cliff is 35 metres high, so we can write

$$s = 4.9t^2 \quad (t \geq 0, \; s \leq 35),$$

and this defines fully the extent to which the equation is valid within the model.

The final part of this stage of the modelling cycle is to recast the two questions from Stage 1 in mathematical terms. These are restated as follows.

(i) Find t when s is 35.

(ii) Find an expression for the instantaneous velocity, $v\,\mathrm{m\,s}^{-1}$, and use this expression to find the value of v when t has the value found from Question (i).

Now we are ready to work on Stage 3, which consists of 'doing the maths'. Finding the answer to Question (i) is straightforward. Starting from the equation

$$s = 4.9t^2 \quad (t \geq 0, \; s \leq 35),$$

we substitute $s = 35$ and solve for t. We find that

$$t^2 = \frac{35}{4.9}.$$

Now we have $t \geq 0$, so the positive square root is required here, that is,

We have not rounded the value of t to a 'reasonable' value here; that comes later. This unrounded value will be used to evaluate the answer to Question (ii). It is not advisable to carry forward heavily rounded values in a calculation (though in this case a fewer number of decimal places than shown would in fact be adequate).

$$t = \sqrt{\frac{35}{4.9}} = 2.672\,612\ldots.$$

In order to answer Question (ii), we need to differentiate the equation for s, which can now be written with both of the limitations on t, as

$$s = 4.9t^2 \quad (0 \leq t \leq 2.672\,612\ldots).$$

The derivative of s with respect to t is

$$\frac{ds}{dt} = 4.9 \times 2t = 9.8t \quad (0 \leq t \leq 2.672\,612\ldots),$$

so that the velocity v is given by

$$v = 9.8t \quad (0 \leq t \leq 2.672\,612\ldots).$$

Now we require a value for v when $t = 2.672\,612\ldots$, which is

$$v = 9.8 \times 2.672\,612\ldots = 26.191\,601\ldots.$$

These calculations complete Stage 3 of the modelling cycle, and we therefore move on to Stage 4 and interpret the results. This is the stage where the variables t and v are related back to the actual physical quantities which they represent, and also where the calculated values are rounded to a number of significant figures which is 'reasonable' in terms of the assumptions made and consistent with the accuracy of any input data.

It is certainly inappropriate to quote the results to seven or eight significant figures. As already noted, the rock may be spinning and there will in fact be some air resistance. In any case, the value which was used for the acceleration due to gravity (the 'input data' in this case) is accurate to only two significant figures, so it is unreasonable to give the answers to a greater level of accuracy than this. Hence we should quote the final predictions of the model to no more than two significant figures, and even then it would be safest to preface these values with the word 'about'. Thus the model predicts that

◇   the rock takes about 2.7 seconds to fall from the top of the cliff to the ground;

◇   when it hits the ground, it is travelling at about $26 \, \mathrm{m \, s}^{-1}$.

$26 \, \mathrm{m \, s}^{-1}$ is nearly 60 mph.

The final stage in the modelling cycle is to evaluate the outcome. The assumptions made at the start would not lead anyone to expect that the calculated results are very accurate predictions of what will actually occur. However, the producer can deduce from the model that the rock will take 2 to 3 seconds to fall, rather than 1 second or 10 seconds, and similarly he has an approximate idea of its final speed.

That is as far as we shall take this model for the falling rock, but there are two related points worth noting. In Stage 3 of the modelling cycle, we arrived at the equation

$$v = \frac{ds}{dt} = 9.8t$$

(leaving aside the precise restrictions on the values of t for which this is valid). If we now differentiate this equation again, then we find that the acceleration $a \, \mathrm{m \, s}^{-2}$ of the rock while it falls is given by

$$a = \frac{dv}{dt} = \frac{d^2s}{dt^2} = 9.8.$$

This value is just the acceleration due to gravity, as indeed it should be.

The other matter to be noted concerns our choice of the origin for displacement measurements and of the positive direction along the vertical line of the motion. We took the top of the cliff as the origin and chose the downward direction as positive. However, an alternative and equally valid choice would have been to take the origin at the *foot* of the cliff (at ground level) and to regard the *upward* direction as positive.

In fact, you will see in Chapter C2 that the equation $s = \frac{1}{2}gt^2$ can be *derived* from taking the acceleration of the object to be $a = g$.

Suppose that this choice is made, and let h metres denote the displacement of the rock with respect to this origin and positive direction. Then h and s are related by

$$h = 35 - s,$$

Here h stands for 'height above the ground'.

because the cliff is 35 metres high. The equation for h in terms of t is therefore (again dispensing with the limits on values of t)

$$h = 35 - 4.9t^2.$$

If we now differentiate this equation for h, then we obtain

$$\frac{dh}{dt} = -4.9 \times 2t = -9.8t,$$

which will be *negative* for positive values of t. Why is this so?

The answer is that the positive direction is now defined as upwards. The minus sign in the velocity, dh/dt, tells us that the stone is moving in the opposite direction, that is, downwards. Similarly, on differentiating once more, we find that

$$\frac{d^2h}{dt^2} = -9.8,$$

and again there is a minus sign, because the acceleration is directed downwards while the positive direction has been chosen as upwards.

Activity 4.6   Taking a bungee jump

Have you ever wondered how fast people fall during a bungee jump, before the bungee starts to pull against gravity? This activity invites you to apply the standard model introduced above to this situation in order to find out.

(a) Consider the assumptions of the standard model that (i) there is no air resistance, and (ii) the object starts its fall from rest. Are these likely to be as valid here as in the case of the falling rock, and if so, why?

(b) In a particular bungee jump the rope (bungee) is 25 metres long when unstretched, and the jump starts from the point at which one end of the rope is fixed (the other end is attached to the person who jumps). Estimate the speed of the jumper at the moment when they stop falling freely and begin to have their downward motion restrained by the rope.

Comment

Solutions are given on page 81.

Summary of Section 4

This section has shown how differentiation may be employed in the analysis of one-dimensional motion, and in particular introduced a standard model for the motion of an object which falls vertically.

◇   The *displacement* s of an object moving along a straight line is a measure of how far it is from a fixed point (*origin*) on the line and of its direction relative to that point. The magnitude $|s|$ of the displacement is the *distance* of the object from the fixed point.

◇   Given an expression for the displacement s in terms of time t, the *velocity* v of the object is the rate of change of displacement with respect to time, that is,

$$v = \frac{ds}{dt}.$$

The sign of v indicates the direction in which the object is moving. The magnitude $|v|$ of the velocity is the *speed* of the object.

◇   The *acceleration* a of the object is the rate of change of its velocity with respect to time,

$$a = \frac{dv}{dt},$$

and the direction of a is indicated by its sign. The acceleration can also be expressed in terms of the displacement s, as

$$a = \frac{d^2 s}{dt^2},$$

which is the *second derivative* of s with respect to t. This is denoted by $\ddot{s}$ in Newton's notation and by $f''(t)$ in function notation (where $s = f(t)$).

◇   There is a standard model which can be used when modelling the motion of objects falling vertically. This features the equation

$$s = \tfrac{1}{2}gt^2,$$

where s is the displacement of the object from its starting point (with the downward direction taken as positive), t is time since the start of the motion and g is the acceleration due to gravity ($9.8\,\mathrm{m\,s^{-2}}$ near the surface of the Earth). This result is valid if the object starts from rest, there are no forces other than gravity acting on it (in particular, air resistance is ignored), the object is not spinning and the fall takes place in calm, wind-free conditions.

Exercise for Section 4

Exercise 4.1

Without using Mathcad, find the second derivative of each of the functions given in Exercise 3.1 on page 40.

5 Optimisation

A calculator will be helpful in studying much of this section. You will need access to your computer, together with Computer Book C, in order to study Subsection 5.3.

If you divide your study of the section between two sessions, then a good place to break off is at the end of Subsection 5.2. You will not then need to use your computer in the first of these two study sessions.

5.1 Maxima and minima

In Section 4 differentiation was applied only in situations which involve motion. As mentioned earlier in the chapter, modelling with continuous variables is not confined to describing moving objects, and differentiation can be used to find the instantaneous rate of change of any variable with respect to any related variable.

There is one procedure using differentiation which has wide applicability, and this procedure is the main subject of this section. It concerns the requirement to locate an *optimum* value for a function, where 'optimum' usually means one of 'highest' or 'lowest' or 'largest' or 'smallest'. Which of these possible meanings applies will depend on the situation being modelled and on the purpose of the model.

For example, suppose that a manufacturing company wants to find a sale price for their goods which makes their profit as large as possible. This would be referred to as *maximising* their profit. As another example, a car owner may wish to replace her current car with another of an age which will keep the running costs as low as possible. This would be referred to as *minimising* the running costs. A third example is provided by the aim of traffic planners to design a new road system in such a way that, by regulation of the vehicles' speed, the traffic flow is made as large as possible. This would be referred to as *maximising* the traffic flow.

Finding an optimum value therefore means finding either a maximum or a minimum value, depending on the situation.

How can differentiation help with this aim? Look at Figure 5.1. The important feature here is that both at a maximum point on a curve and at a minimum point, the gradient is zero. You know from earlier in the chapter that differentiation is used to find the gradients at points on curves, so it seems reasonable to use differentiation now to find where the gradient of a particular curve is zero.

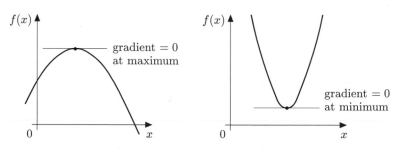

Figure 5.1

This is not quite the whole story, though. If the independent variable arises from some feature of a real situation which is being modelled, then there are normally limitations on the values which this variable can take within the model. Such a limitation can alter matters, as Figure 5.2 illustrates.

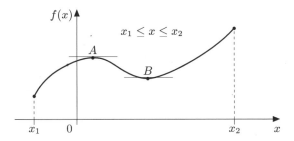

Figure 5.2

In Figure 5.2, there are two points where the curve has a gradient of zero, namely, A and B. However, the highest point on the curve in the interval between x_1 and x_2 is not at either of A or B, but rather at the end-point where $x = x_2$. Similarly, the lowest point on the curve in this interval is not at A or B, but at the end-point where $x = x_1$.

The two points on the graph of Figure 5.2 where the gradient is zero are called respectively a *local maximum* (A) and a *local minimum* (B). Other terms used for both local maxima and local minima are *stationary points* and *turning points.*

The plural of 'maximum' is 'maxima', and the plural of 'minimum' is 'minima'.

To be more precise, a **stationary point** is any point on a graph at which the gradient (derivative) is zero. This includes all local maxima and minima but, as you will see shortly, these are not the only possibilities.

Differentiation followed by setting the derivative equal to zero will always locate any stationary points on a graph. Whether one of these is the overall maximum or minimum which is sought within a model depends both on the shape of the curve and on any restrictions which apply to the range of values of the independent variable.

Activity 5.1   Identifying maxima and minima

For each of the graphs (a) and (b) in Figure 5.3 below, identify:

(a) any local maxima or local minima;

(b) the overall maximum for the interval shown;

(c) the overall minimum for the interval shown.

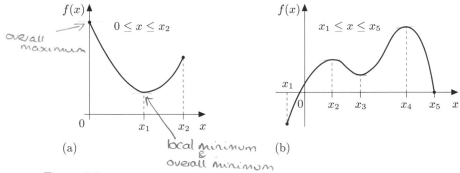

Figure 5.3

Comment

Solutions are given on page 82.

We next summarise the procedure for finding an overall maximum or minimum.

> **Optimisation procedure**
> To find the highest (or lowest) value of a smooth function $f(x)$ over an interval of values of the variable x, the procedure is as follows.
> (i) Differentiate the function $f(x)$ to obtain the derivative $f'(x)$.
> (ii) Solve the equation $f'(x) = 0$, in order to find all the values of x within the given interval at which there might be a local maximum or local minimum.
> (iii) Find the value of $f(x)$ at each of these values of x.
> (iv) Find also the value of $f(x)$ at each end of the interval of values for x.
> (v) If seeking an overall maximum, choose the highest value of $f(x)$ from those obtained in Steps (iii) and (iv). If seeking an overall minimum, choose the lowest value of $f(x)$ from those obtained in Steps (iii) and (iv).

Example 5.1 Finding the highest value

Find the highest value of the function

$$f(x) = \tfrac{1}{3}x^3 - x^2 - 8x + 1 \quad (-3 \le x \le 5),$$

within the range of values given for x.

Solution

We apply the five-step procedure above.

Step (i): This function can be differentiated 'by hand', to give

$$f'(x) = x^2 - 2x - 8.$$

Step (ii): On setting this expression equal to zero, we have the equation

$$x^2 - 2x - 8 = 0.$$

By factorising the left-hand side, to obtain

$$(x + 2)(x - 4) = 0,$$

or by applying the solution formula for quadratic equations, we find the two solutions

$$x = -2 \quad \text{and} \quad x = 4.$$

Note that both of these values are within the stated interval for x.

Step (iii): The corresponding values for $f(x)$ are

$$f(-2) = \tfrac{1}{3} \times (-2)^3 - (-2)^2 - 8 \times (-2) + 1$$
$$= -\tfrac{8}{3} - 4 + 16 + 1$$
$$= 10\tfrac{1}{3}$$

and

$$f(4) = \tfrac{1}{3} \times 4^3 - 4^2 - 8 \times 4 + 1$$
$$= \tfrac{64}{3} - 16 - 32 + 1$$
$$= -25\tfrac{2}{3}.$$

Step (iv): The values for $f(x)$ at the two end-points are

$$f(-3) = \tfrac{1}{3} \times (-3)^3 - (-3)^2 - 8 \times (-3) + 1$$
$$= -9 - 9 + 24 + 1$$
$$= 7$$

and

$$f(5) = \tfrac{1}{3} \times 5^3 - 5^2 - 8 \times 5 + 1$$
$$= \tfrac{125}{3} - 25 - 40 + 1$$
$$= -22\tfrac{1}{3}.$$

Step (v): The highest value of $f(x)$ from those calculated in Steps (iii) and (iv) is $10\tfrac{1}{3}$ (at $x = -2$). This is therefore the highest value of the function in the given range.

Activity 5.2   Finding lowest values

Find the lowest value of each of the following functions within the range of values given for the independent variable. (Note that all of these functions can be differentiated 'by hand'.)

(a) $f(x) = 3x^2 - 2x + 5$ $(-1 \le x \le 4)$;

(b) $f(t) = 6 + 4t - t^2$ $(-1 \le t \le 1)$;

(c) $f(y) = ay^2 + by + c$ $\left(-\dfrac{b}{a} \le y \le 0\right)$, where a and b are positive constants and c is a constant.

Comment

Solutions are given on page 82.

5.2   How much profit can you make?

In this section we develop a simple model which uses the idea of finding an optimum value.

Imagine that you have a hobby which involves making something, say, child-sized painted wooden stools, dolls dressed in replica period costumes, garden gnomes or embroidered place-mats. The choice is yours, but it will help to think of an item which could perhaps sell for a price in the range of £12 to £20. Now suppose that you are considering how much extra income can be made from selling these items which you make. More precisely, since making them also involves some financial outlay, you would like to know how much *profit* you can make. In fact, you want to find out how to maximise your profit by choosing a suitable selling price for your product.

It is appropriate to regard the £12 as including the cost of the time which it takes you to make each item.

Imagine that the materials required to make your product cost £12 for each item, and that there is also a small monthly fixed cost of £20, which represents your overheads. You would therefore have to charge a little over £12 in order to make any profit at all.

Your first thought might be to set the price at a high level (well over £12), but there will surely be some limit to what people are prepared to pay. Suppose that, after carrying out a small survey of interest at your local market, you come to the conclusion that no one would be prepared to buy your product at a price over £20, and that many fewer people would buy at a price close to £20 than if the item was priced near £12. This suggests that you might make a larger profit by selling more items at a lower price rather than a few at a higher price.

On this basis, you decide to do some mathematical modelling. In what follows we refer again to the diagram of the modelling cycle (Figure 4.4 on page 51).

In order to start modelling you need to identify the purpose of your model. This is:

◇   to find a selling price for each item that you make in order to maximise your profit.

In moving to Stage 2 of the modelling process (creating the model), you need to draw on some standard formulas relating to prices and profits. These are:

Here *revenue* means 'income from sale of some items', and *costs* means 'how much is spent to produce those items'.

profit = revenue − costs;

revenue = selling price per item × number of items sold.

You need to measure all of these quantities over the same time interval. For instance, if you want to calculate how much profit you can make each month, then you need to consider your monthly revenue and your monthly costs.

Suppose that you do decide to work on a monthly basis. You might then define the following quantities:

£M is the monthly profit;

£R is the monthly revenue;

£P is the selling price per item;

Q is the quantity of items to be made and sold each month;

£C is the cost of making these Q items.

Notice that there is an assumption implicit in the definition of Q:

◇   that all the items which you make in a month are sold in that month.

(If this were not the case, then of course you would incur costs in a month without the receipt of corresponding income, and taking that into account would make the model more complicated. This is therefore a convenient assumption to make in order to simplify the model.)

In terms of the symbols just defined, the two standard formulas relating prices and profits may be expressed as

$$M = R - C,$$
$$R = PQ.$$

You are interested in how your profit depends upon the selling price of each item, since the specified purpose of the model is to find a selling price for each item which maximises the profit. In order to relate the profit to the selling price, you need to find how each of Q and C is related to P.

Activity 5.3   Reflection

Satisfy yourself that, if you know how Q and C are related to P, that is, if you have an equation for Q in terms of P and another for C in terms of P, then you will be able to write down an equation for M in terms of P.

Comment

From the standard relations given above you can write

$$M = PQ - C.$$

Now if you have equations which relate Q to P and C to P, then you can substitute for the Q and the C in the above equation to obtain an equation for M which has P as the only independent variable.

The survey which you carried out showed that the quantity of items which you could sell falls off as the price is raised, and that none would be sold once the price passes £20. Suppose that, on the basis of the same survey, you estimate that you can probably sell about 80 items per month if they are priced at £12. You decide on this basis to use the following linear equation to describe how the quantity of items you can sell each month, Q, depends on the price at which you sell them, £P:

$$Q = 200 - 10P \quad (12 \leq P \leq 20).$$

Here the limitations $12 \leq P \leq 20$ are imposed because you make no money at all out of the venture if you sell at under £12, and £20 seems to be the highest price which the market will bear.

Notice that another assumption has just been made:

◇   that the quantity sold varies linearly with selling price.

Probably the variation is not perfectly linear, but this equation does have the merit of being simple and hence easy to handle.

Question: Is this linear equation consistent with the conclusions reached from the survey?

Answer: Yes, because $Q = 80$ when $P = 12$, and $Q = 0$ when $P = 20$.

Your monthly costs, £C, are the sum of a £20 fixed cost and £12 for each item made, giving the equation

$$C = 20 + 12Q.$$

Question: How can this equation be rewritten in terms of P rather than Q?

Answer: By using the equation above which relates Q to P.

This step leads to

$$C = 20 + 12(200 - 10P)$$
$$= 2420 - 120P \quad (12 \leq P \leq 20).$$

Your monthly revenue, £R, is the quantity which you sell each month multiplied by the price of each item, that is,

$$R = (200 - 10P)P$$
$$= 200P - 10P^2 \quad (12 \leq P \leq 20).$$

You may feel that it is inappropriate to treat Q as a continuous rather than a discrete variable. However, this approach allows differentiation to be used, which in turn leads to an optimisation procedure, so it is convenient to regard Q as a continuous variable.

As an exercise, you might try to derive the equation of the line from this information.

It is now possible to write down an equation which relates your monthly profit from the venture to the selling price of your items:

$$M = R - C$$
$$= 200P - 10P^2 - (2420 - 120P)$$
$$= -10P^2 + 320P - 2420 \quad (12 \le P \le 20).$$

Here M, the monthly profit in pounds, is a function of P, the selling price of each item in pounds. As the price varies, so does the profit. This is exactly the equation needed to permit investigation of how the profit may be maximised.

The stage of creating the model is almost complete. It remains only to re-state the original purpose of the model in mathematical terms. A suitable formulation is as follows.

◇   Is there a value of P which maximises

$$M = -10P^2 + 320P - 2420 \quad (12 \le P \le 20),$$

and if so, what is it?

Activity 5.4   Reflection

Check that this question is the mathematical equivalent of the model's purpose as identified in Stage 1 of the modelling process.

Comment

Notice how the question recasts the purpose (finding a price to maximise your profit) in terms of the variables and equation arrived at in Stage 2 of the modelling cycle. It is always advisable to change the original question in this way at the end of Stage 2, because doing so focuses your thoughts on exactly what is needed in Stage 3 (doing the maths).

In order to carry out Stage 3, we shall need the Optimisation Procedure which was introduced in Subsection 5.1 (page 58).

Try not to be confused between the numbered stages of the modelling cycle and the numbered steps from the Optimisation Procedure!

The first step in this procedure is to differentiate the function. On differentiating the equation

$$M = -10P^2 + 320P - 2420 \quad (12 \le P \le 20),$$

we obtain

$$\frac{dM}{dP} = -20P + 320 \quad (12 \le P \le 20).$$

The second step is to solve the equation $dM/dP = 0$, that is,

$$-20P + 320 = 0.$$

The solution is

$$P = 16.$$

This value of P lies within the specified interval ($12 \le P \le 20$), so the original function has a stationary value in the range of interest.

Step (iii) is to find the value of M at this value of P, giving

$$M = -10 \times 16^2 + 320 \times 16 - 2420$$
$$= 140.$$

Next is Step (iv), which is to check the values of M at the two end-points of the range. Here the ends are at $P = 12$ and $P = 20$. At $P = 12$ we have

$$M = -10 \times 12^2 + 320 \times 12 - 2420$$
$$= -20.$$

Similarly, at $P = 20$ we find that

$$M = -10 \times 20^2 + 320 \times 20 - 2420$$
$$= -20.$$

So (Step (v) of the procedure) M is largest at $P = 16$, when it has the value 140.

That concludes Stage 3 of the modelling cycle. Stage 4 requires interpretation of the results. Here you need to remember that P stands for the selling price in pounds for each item, and M, also in pounds, stands for your monthly profit. The model suggests that your best approach is to sell at £16 per item in order to make a monthly profit of £140. There are assumptions underlying the model, so these values are only estimates.

There is one other thing that you need to know, which did not feature in the original question but whose importance now becomes apparent.

Question: Can you see what this is?

Answer: You need to know what quantity to sell at the price of £16, because this is the number of items you will make!

Reverting to Stage 3, the equation relating Q to P is

$$Q = 200 - 10P \quad (12 \le P \le 20),$$

and if $P = 16$ then

$$Q = 200 - (10 \times 16) = 40.$$

Interpreting this result (Stage 4 again), the model suggests that you should make 40 items each month.

In evaluating the outcome, only you can decide whether the potential profit will make the required effort worthwhile! As for the model itself, you might need to look again at the way costs are modelled. Is there something else which should have been included? The survey which was conducted to estimate how the number of items you could sell varies with price might merit further scrutiny. How reliable are the data which you obtained? Is the linear equation relating Q to P an adequate description of what you found? Is it worth undertaking a further investigation to confirm the first impressions?

Alternatively, you might just decide to go ahead with the project and try selling at various prices around the £16 mark, settling on the price which actually provides the most profit.

5.3 Using Mathcad in optimisation

Note that you will need access to your computer, together with Computer Book C, in order to study this subsection.

As you studied Subsections 5.1 and 5.2, it may have occurred to you that much of the detailed work could be carried out using Mathcad. You are now invited to explore the extent to which this is the case, and in particular to find where Mathcad can assist with the Optimisation Procedure described in Subsection 5.1 (page 58).

The first application of Mathcad is to the calculation which you carried out in Subsection 5.2, in the context of a model developed to maximise profit. This is followed by a slightly more complicated optimisation problem which could arise from a revision of that model.

Refer to Computer Book C for the work in this subsection.

In this computer session, you saw that Mathcad can be used in the following ways with the Optimisation Procedure:

◇   finding the derivative of the function whose value is to be maximised or minimised (Step (i));

◇   solving the equation which results from setting this derivative equal to zero (Step (ii));

◇   evaluating the original function at any given value of the independent variable (Steps (iii) and (iv)).

If you adopt this graphical approach for any of the functions considered so far in this subsection, you will find that it confirms the results which were obtained through use of the Optimisation Procedure.

For the examples we have looked at, Mathcad can also be used to plot a graph of the function and zoom in on areas of interest. A similar facility is present on graphics calculators. This raises the question of why we do not rely solely on the graph of a function, and read off the maximum or minimum value in the range of interest.

You saw parameters (in this sense) mentioned first in Chapter A1, Subsection 4.2. They were referred to in a modelling context in Chapter B2, Subsection 1.2.

The answer is that optimisation problems involving two main variables may also feature parameters which, although regarded as constant for the purposes of the optimisation, do not have specific numerical values associated with them. You saw an example of such a situation in Activity 5.2(c), where values were not given for the three constants a, b and c in the equation

$$f(y) = ay^2 + by + c \quad \left(-\frac{b}{a} \le y \le 0 \right).$$

The presence of parameters permits more general problems to be stated and solved. In finding the minimum value of the function above in terms of the three constants, you solved in effect an infinite number of optimisation problems, each with different values for the three constants.

If you have the time, you might like to try using Mathcad in the process of minimising the expression $f(y)$ above.

The symbolic processor in Mathcad may be used to deal with such cases. However, a graphical approach will not work, since Mathcad can produce the graph of an equation which relates two variables only when the values of any constants in that equation have been specified. The upshot of these remarks is that the Optimisation Procedure of Subsection 5.1 remains useful despite the graphical facilities of Mathcad and of graphics calculators.

5.4 Identifying local maxima and minima

The Optimisation Procedure which you used in Subsections 5.1 to 5.3 identifies the highest or lowest value of any smooth function within an interval of values of the independent variable, whether this optimum value occurs at a stationary point within the interval or at one of its end-points. Sometimes, however, it is necessary to find out rather more about a function f than where its overall maximum or minimum is. Depending on the modelling interpretation of f, it may be that you are interested in values of x which are well away from local maxima or minima of $f(x)$, or that interest covers the entire range of responses from f.

In such cases, one needs a fuller picture of how the graph of the function behaves. If the function has no parameters in its description, then Mathcad can be used directly to draw the graph over any interval of interest. However, if parameters are present then, as pointed out at the end of the previous subsection, direct plotting is not an option. Even without the presence of parameters, it may be that the overall behaviour of a function can be ascertained rapidly without the use of Mathcad. A rough sketch of the graph will not give accurate numerical values, but may still provide all of the qualitative information that is required.

In these circumstances, where one seeks to establish the overall behaviour of a graph without using Mathcad, it is helpful to be able to classify the stationary points, that is, to decide whether each such point is a local maximum or a local minimum, or perhaps neither of these.

One approach to this task is simply to evaluate values of the function at the stationary point and at a short distance to either side of it. Suppose that the function f has a stationary point at $x = x_1$, and that the values of $f(x)$ at a pair of points on either side of $x = x_1$ (but sufficiently close to it) are both less than $f(x_1)$. Then $x = x_1$ gives a local maximum of f (see Figure 5.4(a)). On the other hand, if the values of $f(x)$ at such a pair of points on either side of $x = x_1$ are both greater than $f(x_1)$, then $x = x_1$ gives a local minimum of f (see Figure 5.4(b)).

Here the extra points are 'sufficiently close' to $x = x_1$ provided that no further stationary point intervenes between them. The same applies in the First Derivative Test below.

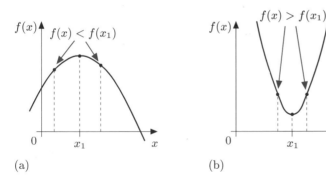

(a)

(b)

Figure 5.4

This approach is straightforward to describe. However, there are two other tests for classifying stationary points which may be easier to apply in practice. These depend on the behaviour of the derivative of the function f near the stationary point $x = x_1$, and the first of them is as follows.

> **First Derivative Test**
>
> Suppose that $x = x_1$ is a stationary point of the smooth function f (so that $f'(x_1) = 0$).
>
> ◇ Find the values of $f'(x)$ at points on either side of $x = x_1$ but sufficiently close to it.
>
> ◇ If these values show $f'(x)$ to be positive to the left of $x = x_1$ and negative to the right, then f has a local maximum at $x = x_1$.
>
> ◇ If these values show $f'(x)$ to be negative to the left of $x = x_1$ and positive to the right, then f has a local minimum at $x = x_1$.

To see why this test works, consider the diagrams below. For a maximum (Figure 5.5(a)), the gradient of the graph of f is positive to the left of the stationary point $x = x_1$ and negative to the right, that is,

$$f'(x) > 0 \text{ for } x < x_1 \quad \text{and} \quad f'(x) < 0 \text{ for } x > x_1.$$

For a minimum (Figure 5.5(b)), the gradient of the graph of f is negative to the left of $x = x_1$ and positive to the right, that is,

$$f'(x) < 0 \text{ for } x < x_1 \quad \text{and} \quad f'(x) > 0 \text{ for } x > x_1.$$

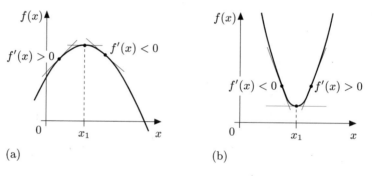

(a) (b)

Figure 5.5

It could be that neither of the situations above applies at a stationary point. For example, the function $f(x) = x^3$ has a stationary point at $x = 0$, but this is neither a maximum nor a minimum (see Figure 5.6).

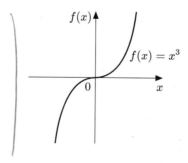

Figure 5.6

The stationary point at $x = 0$ is an example of a *point of inflection.* If a stationary point $x = x_1$ of a function f is a point of inflection then, either values of $f'(x)$ are positive on either side of $x = x_1$ (as in Figure 5.6), or they are negative on either side.

Another test for local maxima or minima involves the second derivative of the function, as follows.

A *point of inflection* $x = x_2$ on the graph of a function f is a point at which the graph alters from being 'concave up' to 'concave down', or vice versa. In other words, it is a local maximum or minimum of the derived function f', so that $f''(x_2) = 0$ and $f''(x)$ changes sign as x increases through x_2. Such a point may or may not also be a stationary point.

Second Derivative Test

Suppose that $x = x_1$ is a stationary point of the smooth function f (so that $f'(x_1) = 0$).

◇ Differentiate $f'(x)$ to obtain an expression for $f''(x)$.

◇ Evaluate $f''(x_1)$.

◇ If $f''(x_1)$ is negative, then f has a local maximum at $x = x_1$.

◇ If $f''(x_1)$ is positive, then f has a local minimum at $x = x_1$.

◇ If $f''(x_1)$ is zero, then the test fails, since the second derivative can be zero at any of a local maximum, a local minimum or a point of inflection.

This test works (when $f''(x_1) \neq 0$) because the second derivative, $f''(x)$, is the derivative or rate-of-change function of the first derivative $f'(x)$. Hence, if $f''(x_1) < 0$, then $f'(x)$ is a decreasing function in the vicinity of $x = x_1$. If also $f'(x_1) = 0$, then we have $f'(x) > 0$ for values of x just less than x_1, and $f'(x) < 0$ for values of x just greater than x_1. It follows from the First Derivative Test that f has a local maximum at $x = x_1$.

A similar argument applies in the case when $f''(x_1) > 0$, for which f' is an increasing function close to $x = x_1$. If also $f'(x_1) = 0$, then the First Derivative Test shows that f has a local minimum at $x = x_1$.

We illustrate how these derivative tests work by applying each of them to the function

$$f(x) = -10x^2 + 320x - 2420.$$

In fact, you already know that this function has a local maximum at $x = 16$, because this is just a version of the 'profit equation' from Subsection 5.2, with x in place of P and without any limitations on the values of x.

Example 5.2   Applying the derivative tests

Classify any stationary points of the function

$$f(x) = -10x^2 + 320x - 2420,$$

using in turn

(a) the First Derivative Test;

(b) the Second Derivative Test.

Solution

Each of the tests applies to stationary points, so we need to start by identifying where these are. The first derivative of $f(x)$ is

$$f'(x) = -20x + 320,$$

Here 16 takes the place of x_1 in the two derivative tests.

and the equation $f'(x) = 0$ has the single solution $x = 16$. This is, therefore, the only stationary point.

(a) .In the absence of any other stationary point, there is no restriction on where we choose the extra points either side to be. For simplicity, we evaluate f' at the integer values $x = 15$ and $x = 17$. This gives

$$f'(15) = -20 \times 15 + 320 = 20$$

and

$$f'(17) = -20 \times 17 + 320 = -20.$$

The gradient is positive to the left of the stationary point and negative to its right, which is the case illustrated in Figure 5.5(a). According to the First Derivative Test, the stationary point at $x = 16$ is a local maximum.

(b) The second derivative of $f(x)$ is obtained by differentiating

$$f'(x) = -20x + 320,$$

and is

$$f''(x) = -20.$$

This is always negative, no matter what value x takes, because it is independent of x. In particular, it is negative at $x = 16$ so that, according to the Second Derivative Test, this corresponds to a local maximum.

Activity 5.7 Applying the derivative tests

This is the function which you considered in Activity 5.2(a).

Classify any stationary points of the function

$$f(x) = 3x^2 - 2x + 5,$$

using in turn

(a) the First Derivative Test;

(b) the Second Derivative Test.

Comment

Solutions are given on page 83.

5.5   *What age of car should Jim buy?*

In this final subsection you are invited to work in stages through a model that uses optimisation. Please pause at each activity and respond to it before reading on. You will find that the material which follows each activity builds on the answer to that activity.

A similar situation to the one described here has been modelled using sequences in Chapter B2 Section 1. Both the discrete model there and the continuous model here have their advantages and drawbacks. You might like to consider what these are as you study this subsection.

Suppose that you have a friend called Jim who is coming to the UK for a year and will need a car. The desired make and model have already been chosen, but Jim wants to decide the age of the car on the basis of the costs of running it for a year. These costs are to be kept as low as possible.

At the end of the year, Jim will sell the car, so one of the costs over the year will be the difference between the price paid for the car and what it can be sold for. This cost is the *depreciation* in the value of the car over the year.

Newer cars have a much higher rate of depreciation than older cars but, on the other hand, newer cars usually have lower repair bills than older ones. So there is a trade-off to be analysed here, and Jim is hoping to select a car by its age so as to exploit this trade-off to the full and minimise costs for the year.

The description so far constitutes the background to Stage 1 of the modelling cycle (see Figure 4.4 on page 51).

Activity 5.8   *Purpose of model*

What, exactly, is the purpose of the model?

Comment

A solution is given on page 83.

In order to set up the model, think about the costs of running a car for one year. These costs are of four types: the depreciation costs, the repair and maintenance costs, the tax and insurance costs and the petrol costs.

Let us choose variables to represent these quantities, as follows:

 £D: the cost of depreciation over one year;

 £R: the cost of repairs and maintenance for one year;

 £T: the tax and insurance costs for one year;

 £P: the petrol costs for one year;

 £C: the total costs for one year.

One other relevant quantity is:

 A years: the age of the car when bought.

Of these, the tax and insurance costs and the petrol costs seem to be more or less independent of the age of the car, and so would not affect the choice of what age of car to buy. On the other hand, the costs of depreciation and of repairs and maintenance depend significantly on the age of the car. We therefore need to find how they depend on the age of the car when bought.

Consider first the annual repair and maintenance costs. Suppose that you have another friend with the same model of car, who has owned it for a number of years since new and who lets you have a look at her records of running costs for the car. In order to see how her repair and maintenance costs relate to the age of the car, you might well plot a graph.

Activity 5.9   Repair and maintenance costs

Suppose that the running costs for each year are represented by the plotted points in Figure 5.7, where the cost $£R$ in each case is for the year which starts at the corresponding age A. Suppose also that you have fitted the line shown to these points. What is the equation of this line, and what limitations on the value of A should be specified in connection with this equation?

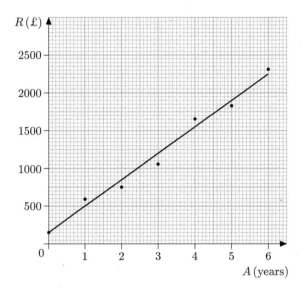

Figure 5.7

Comment

Solutions are given on page 83.

Now consider the annual costs of depreciation. Data on these costs can be obtained from booklets of used-car costs which are sold by newsagents. The depreciation over one year is just the difference between the cost of buying a car of one age and selling a car of one year older, so it is a straightforward matter to deduce data which relate D and A. As you might expect, D decreases as A increases, because there is less depreciation on an older car. Also, D decreases faster when A is small than when A is larger (younger cars depreciate faster). Suppose that a plot of such data for the model of car under investigation produces the graph of Figure 5.8. It looks as if these data points could be approximated by the graph of a decaying exponential function, and indeed it turns out that the points are fitted reasonably well by the equation

$$D = 2500 \exp(-0.25A) \quad (0 \le A \le 6).$$

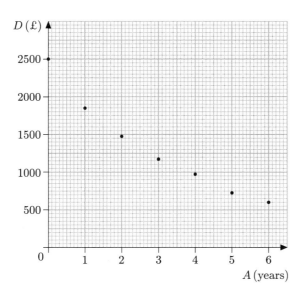

Figure 5.8

Activity 5.10   What assumptions?

Identify all of the assumptions made so far.

Comment

A solution is given on page 83.

To continue with Stage 2 of the modelling process, we need both to find an equation which relates the total cost £C to the car age A years and to identify the mathematical problem to be solved.

Activity 5.11   The mathematical problem

(a) Write down an equation which relates C to A. (This equation will include the constants T and P.)

(b) What is the mathematical problem to be solved?

Comment

Solutions are given on page 83.

This concludes Stage 2 of the modelling cycle. Stage 3 is to do the mathematics, that is, to solve the mathematical problem.

Activity 5.12   Optimisation

Use the process of optimisation to find the value of A which makes C as small as possible. (Note that, since T and P are constants, each has a zero derivative with respect to A.)

Comment

A solution is given on page 84.

This completes Stage 3 of the modelling cycle. The next stage is to interpret this result.

Activity 5.13   Interpretation

Interpret the result which you obtained in Activity 5.12.

Comment

A solution is given on page 84.

Finally, as Stage 5 of the modelling cycle, there is evaluation of the outcome. Some of the assumptions probably need refining. The assumption that repair and maintenance costs increase linearly with age is a bit suspect. Firstly, the data points do not lie exactly on a straight line and, secondly, the car which Jim buys may not behave just like the car from which the data about repair and maintenance costs were gathered. It would not be easy to obtain any more useful data, so this is really a matter of flagging the point and noting that it will make the prediction of the model rather an approximate one.

Similar comments could be made about the exponential decrease of depreciation with the age of car. On the other hand, if you read magazines about buying cars then you will probably have noticed suggestions that one to two years old is a good age at which to buy a car in order to keep costs down. Most people keep a car for longer than the one year stipulated here, so perhaps an age of two to two and a half years at purchase is not too unrealistic.

Activity 5.14   Reflection

Look back at the modelling process which you have just gone through in this subsection. Use your Learning File Sheet 3 to record how you feel about this process.

Comment

Are you feeling more confident about carrying out modelling for yourself? Would you have been able to work through the problem in this subsection with less prompting? If not, can you identify what you would have found hard, and why? Can you work out a strategy for improving your modelling ability and make a pact with yourself to implement it?

Summary of Section 5

This section has shown how differentiation may be used in the process of determining an *optimum* (highest, lowest, largest or smallest) value of a function.

◇ A *stationary point* of a function is a point where the graph of the function has zero gradient. The stationary points of a function $f(x)$ may be found by differentiating and then setting the derivative $f'(x)$ equal to zero. The solutions of the resulting equation are the values of x at which $f(x)$ has stationary points.

◇ The highest (or lowest) value of a smooth function $f(x)$ over an interval of values of the variable x can be found by applying the Optimisation Procedure described on page 58.

◇ There are several ways of determining whether a stationary point is a local maximum, a local minimum, or neither of these. Two useful methods of deciding on the classification of a stationary point are the First Derivative Test (see page 66) and the Second Derivative Test (see page 67).

The section has also demonstrated how the Optimisation Procedure can be used in modelling.

Activity 5.15   Consolidation

In Section 1 it was suggested that you could profitably return to that section after you had studied the rest of this chapter. The suggestion was a serious one; you should find that re-reading that section at this stage enhances your understanding of differentiation. You are therefore encouraged to re-read Section 1 now, if you have the time available to do so. You may also find it useful to look over the notes you made in reponse to Activities 0.1 and 1.2 and see if you wish to add to or otherwise amend them.

Comment

As you study Section 1 again, take the opportunity to reflect on the concept of differentiation as you now understand it. Remember that mental reflection is an active process which involves thinking and trying to reach a deeper insight. You may find it useful to try and explain key ideas out loud, as this helps to bring coherence to your thoughts.

Exercises for Section 5   *not attempted due to lack of time*

Exercise 5.1

(a) Find the coordinates of all stationary points of the function

$$f(x) = 3x^4 - 2x^3 - 9x^2 + 7.$$

(b) Classify each of these stationary points as a local maximum, a local minimum or neither, using in turn

   (i) the First Derivative Test (page 66);

   (ii) the Second Derivative Test (page 67).

Exercise 5.2

The equation

$$h = 30t - 5t^2$$

is to be used as a model for the motion of a ball projected vertically upwards with a particular initial speed. Here h metres is the height above the point of projection and t seconds is the time since the moment of projection.

(a) Express the velocity v m s^{-1} of the ball in terms of t.

(b) What is the speed with which the ball is projected?

(c) What is the maximum height of the ball above its point of projection?

(d) At what times is the ball 25 metres above its point of projection?

Exercise 5.3

A wheat farmer is interested in maximising his profit per hectare. He has discovered through experimentation that the increase in yield falls off markedly as he increases the amount of fertiliser which is applied (see Figure 5.9).

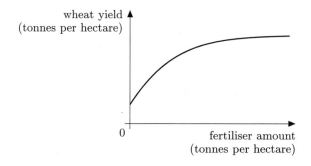

Figure 5.9

Modelling has led him to two equations. His expected revenue per hectare, £R, is related to the amount of fertiliser applied per hectare, T tonnes, by the equation

$$R = 900 - 600 \exp(-5T) \quad (0 \le T \le 1).$$

His costs per hectare, £C, are related to T by the equation

$$C = 100 + 180T \quad (0 \le T \le 1).$$

How much fertiliser should the farmer apply per hectare in order to maximise his profit per hectare, £M? (*Hint*: Remember that profit equals revenue minus costs.)

Exercise 5.4

Traffic planners have developed a simple model to describe how the volume of traffic flow varies with the average speed of the traffic along a road. They want to know whether there is a value of the speed which maximises the traffic flow. If this is the case, then it may be possible to improve the flow by changing the speed limit on the road.

Their model assumes that drivers always maintain a safe stopping distance between their vehicle and the one in front. (Therefore, as the vehicles go faster, the spacing between them increases.) This assumption, together with some appropriate data, leads to the following equation relating the traffic flow rate, F vehicles per second, to the average speed of the traffic, $v \, \mathrm{m\,s^{-1}}$:

$$F = \frac{12v}{v^2 + 12v + 12} \quad (0 \le v \le 30).$$

At what speed will the traffic flow along the road be maximised, in this model?

Hint: According to Mathcad (as you can confirm), the derivative of F with respect to v is

$$\frac{dF}{dv} = -12\frac{(v^2 - 12)}{(v^2 + 12v + 12)^2}.$$

Summary of Chapter C1

The major concepts covered by this chapter are:

◇ what differentiation is (discussed informally in Section 1 and formally in Section 2), and the limit definition of differentiation (Section 2);

◇ how to differentiate functions, either 'by hand' or using Mathcad (Section 3);

◇ how to optimise a function over a range of values of the independent variable, or to find a local maximum or minimum (Section 5);

◇ what differentiation is used for (discussed throughout the chapter, and illustrated in modelling examples in Sections 4 and 5);

◇ how to model problems that involve motion or optimisation (Sections 4 and 5).

Learning outcomes

You have been working towards the following learning outcomes.

Terms to know and use

Gradient, tangent, discrete variable, continuous variable, average rate of change, instantaneous rate of change, differentiation, derived function, derivative, differentiation from first principles, speed, velocity, distance, displacement, acceleration, second derivative, stationary point, turning point, local maximum, local minimum.

Symbols and notation to know and use

The various notations for first and second derivatives:

◇ $f'(x), f''(x)$ (function notation);

◇ $\dfrac{dy}{dx}, \dfrac{d^2y}{dx^2}, \dfrac{d}{dx}(y), \dfrac{d^2}{dx^2}(y)$ (Leibniz notation);

◇ $\dot{s}, \ddot{s}$ (Newton's notation).

The notation for limits, as applied in the definition of the derivative

$$f'(t) = \lim_{h \to 0} \left[\frac{f(t+h) - f(t)}{h} \right].$$

Ideas to be aware of

◇ The difference between average and instantaneous rates of change.

◇ That a smooth curve has a gradient at each point along it, as given by the gradient of the tangent at the point.

◇ That the derived function (derivative) of any smooth function is found by differentiation, and is equivalent both to the gradient function and to the instantaneous rate of change function.

◇ The uses of differentiation.

◇ The difference between speed and velocity, and between distance and displacement.

◇ The concept of an optimum value, and its relationship with the derivative of a function.

◇ What mathematical modelling is, and how the modelling cycle is used.

Mathematical skills

◇ Differentiate 'by hand' any function of a type shown in Table 3.2 on page 38. Also, to be able to differentiate any constant multiple, a sum or difference, or a sum of constant multiples of those same functions.

◇ Use differentiation to find instantaneous rates of change in various situations, including instantaneous speeds or velocities (given displacements) and instantaneous accelerations (given velocities).

◇ Evaluate an instantaneous rate of change at any value of the independent variable.

◇ Use differentiation to find the gradient function of a curve whose equation is known, and evaluate the gradient at any point on the curve.

◇ Use the limit definition of a derived function/derivative to find the derived function/derivative in very simple cases.

◇ Differentiate twice to find second derivatives.

◇ Find the maximum or minimum value of a function in a given range of values of the independent variable.

◇ Apply tests to determine whether a stationary point is a local maximum or a local minimum (or neither).

Mathcad skills

◇ Type expressions to be differentiated (or otherwise manipulated) directly into Mathcad, without the use of a prepared file.

◇ Apply Mathcad to differentiate an expression with respect to a specified variable, by using the d/dx button on the palette and Simplify from the Symbolic menu (or by using Differentiate on Variable from the Symbolic menu).

◇ Use Mathcad to solve an equation for a specified variable using Solve for Variable from the Symbolic menu.

◇ Use Mathcad where appropriate to find second derivatives.

◇ Use the copy and paste facilities in Mathcad.

Modelling skills

Most of these are not new to you, but have been reinforced in this chapter.

◇ Identify the purpose of a model, or the question to be answered.

◇ Make suitable simplifying assumptions.

◇ Identify the variables in a situation and find a suitable equation to relate them.

◇ Express the purpose or question of the model in mathematical terms.

◇ Interpret the mathematical result appropriately, given the assumptions made.

◇ Use modelling to solve simple problems about motion and problems involving optimisation.

Learning skills

These are not new to you, but have been reinforced in this chapter.

◇   Identify terms which are given a special meaning (different from everyday English) and confirm that you understand this special meaning.

◇   Reflect on what you are learning in order to make sense of it.

◇   Identify points which are not clear to you as you study material and find strategies for obtaining clarification.

Investigating processes to aid understanding

◇   Develop a visual sense of what is involved in finding the derivative of a function at a point, and of how the graph of the derivative relates to the graph of the original function.

◇   Apply general results in specific instances and, conversely, use conjecture and test to go from specific instances to a general result.

Solutions to Activities

Solution 1.1

On the first stage the average speed is 1500 metres divided by 120 seconds, which is 12.5 metres per second. On the second stage, the average speed is 400 metres divided by 60 seconds, which is 6.67 metres per second (to two decimal places).

Solution 1.5

(a) (i) Here $t = 3$, so we have
$$v = \frac{2 \times 3}{9}$$
$$= \tfrac{2}{3} \text{ or } 0.67 \text{ (to 2 d.p.)}.$$

Her instantaneous speed is then $0.67 \, \mathrm{m\,s^{-1}}$.

(ii) Here $t = 20$, giving
$$v = \frac{2 \times 20}{9}$$
$$= \tfrac{40}{9} \text{ or } 4.44 \text{ (to 2 d.p.)},$$

so her speed is then $4.44 \, \mathrm{m\,s^{-1}}$.

(b) There are no obvious equalities, but there are some looser relationships which are worth noting. Firstly, the instantaneous speed $\tfrac{2}{3} \, \mathrm{m\,s^{-1}}$ at $t = 3$ is larger than the average speed $\tfrac{1}{3} \, \mathrm{m\,s^{-1}}$ from $t = 0$ to $t = 3$, but smaller than the average speed $1 \, \mathrm{m\,s^{-1}}$ from $t = 3$ to $t = 6$, which is exactly what would be expected for a steadily increasing speed.

The instantaneous speed at $t = 10$ is $2.22 \, \mathrm{m\,s^{-1}}$. This is quite close to the average speed $\tfrac{7}{3} \, \mathrm{m\,s^{-1}}$ in the interval $t = 9$ to $t = 12$, as you'd expect. Similarly, the instantaneous speed $4.44 \, \mathrm{m\,s^{-1}}$ at $t = 20$ is quite close to the average speed $\tfrac{13}{3} \, \mathrm{m\,s^{-1}}$ from $t = 18$ to $t = 21$.

Solution 1.6

Differentiation gives the instantaneous rate at which v is changing with respect to t, that is, the rate at which the speed changes with respect to time. (This rate of change is called the *acceleration*, and will be referred to again later in the chapter.)

Solution 2.1

In Subsection 1.2 it was stated that applying the process of differentiation to
$$s = 100 \sin\left(\frac{\pi t}{60}\right) \quad (0 \le t \le 30)$$

(the distance–time equation for Jenny's jogging) gives
$$v = \frac{5\pi}{3} \cos\left(\frac{\pi t}{60}\right) \quad (0 \le t \le 30)$$

for Jenny's instantaneous speed $v \, \mathrm{m\,s^{-1}}$. This means that the required gradient function g is given by
$$g(t) = \frac{5\pi}{3} \cos\left(\frac{\pi t}{60}\right) \quad (0 \le t \le 30).$$

Solution 2.2

The quotient given is
$$\frac{(20 + h)^2/9 - 20^2/9}{h} = \frac{(20 + h)^2 - 20^2}{9h}$$
$$= \frac{400 + 40h + h^2 - 400}{9h}$$
$$= \frac{40h + h^2}{9h}$$
$$= \frac{h(40 + h)}{9h}.$$

Assuming that h is not zero, this equals
$$\frac{40 + h}{9},$$

whose limit as h tends to zero is $\tfrac{40}{9}$. This verifies that
$$\lim_{h \to 0} \left[\frac{(20 + h)^2/9 - 20^2/9}{h} \right] = \frac{40}{9},$$

as required.

Solution 2.3

If the expression
$$\frac{5\pi}{3} \cos\left(\frac{\pi t}{60}\right)$$

is to be the derivative of
$$f(t) = 100 \sin\left(\frac{\pi t}{60}\right)$$

then, from equation (2.4), it must be the case that
$$\lim_{h \to 0} \frac{1}{h} \left[100 \sin\left(\frac{\pi (t + h)}{60}\right) - 100 \sin\left(\frac{\pi t}{60}\right) \right]$$
$$= \frac{5\pi}{3} \cos\left(\frac{\pi t}{60}\right).$$

Solution 2.4

(a) If the expression $\frac{10}{3}$ is to be the derivative of $f(t) = \frac{10}{3}t$ then, from equation (2.4), it must be the case that

$$\lim_{h \to 0}\left[\frac{\frac{10}{3}(t+h) - \frac{10}{3}t}{h}\right] = \frac{10}{3}.$$

(b) The quotient in the square brackets in the last equation is $\frac{10}{3}h/h = \frac{10}{3}$, which has limit $\frac{10}{3}$ as h tends to zero. Since this equals the right-hand side of the last equation in (a), the outcome for the derivative of $f(t)$ is as claimed earlier in the text.

Solution 2.5

In each case we apply equation (2.4), which is

$$f'(t) = \lim_{h \to 0}\left[\frac{f(t+h) - f(t)}{h}\right].$$

It is simplest to start by considering the expression inside the square brackets, and simplifying this as far as possible before taking the limit.

(a) Since k is a constant, we find that

$$f(t+h) = f(t) = k,$$

so that

$$\frac{f(t+h) - f(t)}{h} = \frac{k - k}{h}$$

$$= \frac{0}{h} = 0.$$

It follows that

$$f'(t) = \lim_{h \to 0}[0] = 0.$$

(b) Here the given function is $f(t) = t$, for which we have

$$f(t+h) = t + h,$$

and hence

$$\frac{f(t+h) - f(t)}{h} = \frac{(t+h) - t}{h}$$

$$= \frac{h}{h} = 1.$$

This expression is independent of h, so that its value remains unchanged as $h \to 0$, that is,

$$f'(t) = \lim_{h \to 0}[1] = 1.$$

(c) For the function $f(t) = t^2$, we obtain

$$f(t+h) = (t+h)^2,$$

and

$$\frac{f(t+h) - f(t)}{h} = \frac{(t+h)^2 - t^2}{h}$$

$$= \frac{t^2 + 2ht + h^2 - t^2}{h}$$

$$= \frac{h(2t + h)}{h}$$

$$= 2t + h.$$

Hence we have

$$f'(t) = \lim_{h \to 0}[2t + h] = 2t.$$

Solution 4.1

(a) By the Constant Multiple Rule, the derivative of $s = \frac{1}{9}t^2$ with respect to t is $\frac{1}{9}$ times the derivative of t^2, which is obtained by putting $n = 2$ in the second row of Table 3.2. Hence we have

$$\frac{ds}{dt} = \frac{1}{9} \times 2t = \frac{2t}{9}.$$

(b) The required derivative is 100 times the derivative of

$$\sin\left(\frac{\pi t}{60}\right),$$

which is in turn obtained from the third row of Table 3.2, with $a = \pi/60$. This gives

$$\frac{ds}{dt} = 100 \times \frac{\pi}{60}\cos\left(\frac{\pi t}{60}\right) = \frac{5\pi}{3}\cos\left(\frac{\pi t}{60}\right).$$

(c) The derivative of $s = \frac{10}{3}t$ with respect to t is $\frac{10}{3}$ times the derivative of t, that is,

$$\frac{ds}{dt} = \frac{10}{3} \times 1 = \frac{10}{3}.$$

Solution 4.2

(a) (i) At A (while moving from M to P), Tom's displacement relative to the origin M is $20\,\mathrm{m}$ and his velocity is $\frac{10}{3}\,\mathrm{m\,s^{-1}}$.

(ii) At B (while moving from M to P), Tom's displacement relative to the origin M is $60\,\mathrm{m}$ and his velocity is $\frac{10}{3}\,\mathrm{m\,s^{-1}}$.

(iii) At C (while moving from P to M), Tom's displacement relative to the origin M is $90\,\mathrm{m}$ and his velocity is $-\frac{10}{3}\,\mathrm{m\,s^{-1}}$.

All of these displacements are positive, because the positive direction is from M towards P, and Tom is always between these two points. The final velocity is negative, because Tom is then jogging from P towards M, which is the negative direction.

(b) His velocity is in each case the same as in part (a), since the choice of positive direction has not been altered. His displacement relative to the origin H at each of the three points is

(i) $-20\,\mathrm{m}$ at A;

(ii) $20\,\mathrm{m}$ at B;

(iii) $50\,\mathrm{m}$ at C.

Notice how shifting the fixed point from which displacements are measured has changed not only the size of the displacements but, in one case, the sign also.

Solution 4.4

In each case, the equation for a is found by differentiating the equation for v with respect to t.

(a) For Mary, we find
$$a = \tfrac{2}{9} \quad (0 \le t \le 30).$$

(b) For Jenny, we have
$$a = \frac{5\pi}{3} \times \left(-\frac{\pi}{60}\right)\sin\left(\frac{\pi t}{60}\right)$$
$$= -\frac{\pi^2}{36}\sin\left(\frac{\pi t}{60}\right) \quad (0 \le t \le 30).$$

(c) Tom's acceleration is
$$a = 0 \quad (0 \le t \le 30).$$

Solution 4.5

(a) (i) The first derivative of
$$s = 8t - 2t^2 \quad (0 \le t \le 2)$$
with respect to t is
$$\frac{ds}{dt} = 8 - 4t \quad (0 \le t \le 2),$$
and so the second derivative is
$$\frac{d^2 s}{dt^2} = -4 \quad (0 \le t \le 2).$$

(ii) The first derivative of
$$y = 30\exp(0.1x)$$
with respect to x is
$$\frac{dy}{dx} = 30 \times 0.1\exp(0.1x) = 3\exp(0.1x),$$
so that the second derivative is
$$\frac{d^2 y}{dx^2} = 3 \times 0.1\exp(0.1x) = 0.3\exp(0.1x).$$

(b) In Newton's notation, the first derivative of
$$x = 2\sin(3t) + 3\cos(3t)$$
with respect to t is
$$\dot{x} = 2 \times 3\cos(3t) + 3 \times (-3)\sin(3t)$$
$$= 6\cos(3t) - 9\sin(3t),$$
and the second derivative is
$$\ddot{x} = 6 \times (-3)\sin(3t) - 9 \times 3\cos(3t)$$
$$= -18\sin(3t) - 27\cos(3t).$$

Solution 4.6

(a) The assumption about no air resistance may be less valid here than for the case of the falling rock, especially if the jumper falls spread-eagled and so has a larger surface area facing the direction of motion on which air resistance can act. Since the activity is called bungee-*jumping*, you might imagine that the jumper does not start with zero velocity (from rest), though in fact these 'jumps' often have almost zero initial velocity. You will need to assume that it is zero here, and that there is no air resistance, in order to be able to use the standard result. Assuming a zero velocity at the start also ensures that the 'jump' will be entirely vertical, which is again essential for the standard result to be valid.

(b) The modelling assumptions required for the bungee jumper while in free fall are similar to those in the text for the falling rock, leaving aside the discussion as in part (a) above of how accurate these assumptions night be. The variables here are the displacement, s metres, and the time t seconds since the jump starts. Suppose that we take the origin for displacement measurements to be the starting point for the jump, and choose the positive direction to be vertically downwards.

Then the equation relating the variables will be the same as for the falling rock, but with one different limitation, since the equation applies only until such time as the bungee becomes taut. This occurs when $s = 25$ (the length of the unstretched rope), so that we have
$$s = 4.9t^2 \quad (t \ge 0,\ s \le 25).$$

The mathematical questions to be answered are as follows.

(i) Find t when s is 25.

(ii) Find an expression for the instantaneous velocity, $v\,\mathrm{m\,s}^{-1}$, and use this expression to find the value of v when t has the value found from Question (i).

To 'do the maths' for Question (i), we proceed as follows. When s is 25, we find that
$$t^2 = \frac{25}{4.9}.$$

Now we have $t \ge 0$, so the positive square root is required here, that is,
$$t = \sqrt{\frac{25}{4.9}} = 2.258\,769\ldots\,.$$

To answer Question (ii), we differentiate the equation for s, to obtain (for $0 \le t \le 2.258\,769\ldots$)
$$v = \frac{ds}{dt} = 4.9 \times 2t = 9.8t.$$

When $t = 2.258\,769\ldots$, the corresponding velocity is

$$v = 9.8 \times 2.258\,769\ldots = 22.135\,943\ldots\,.$$

At the interpretation stage, it can be said that the velocity after a drop of 25 metres will be about $22\,\mathrm{m\,s^{-1}}$. There is no point in trying to give this value to more significant figures, given the assumptions made and the limited accuracy of the value taken for g. At the evaluation stage of the modelling cycle, much the same discussion as for the falling rock applies, with variations as suggested in part (a) above.

Solution 5.1

(a) From the graph shown in Figure 5.3(a) we have the following.

(a) The graph has no local maximum and a local minimum at $x = x_1$.

(b) Its overall maximum on the interval $0 \le x \le x_2$ is at $x = 0$.

(c) Its overall minimum on this interval is at $x = x_1$ (where the local minimum is).

(b) From the graph shown in Figure 5.3(b) we have the following.

(a) The graph has two local maxima, at $x = x_2$ and at $x = x_4$. It also has a local minimum at $x = x_3$.

(b) Its overall maximum on the interval $x_1 \le x \le x_5$ is at $x = x_4$ (which is one of the local maxima).

(c) Its overall minimum on this interval is at $x = x_1$.

Solution 5.2

In each case we follow the Optimisation Procedure of page 58.

(a) The given function is

$$f(x) = 3x^2 - 2x + 5 \quad (-1 \le x \le 4).$$

Step (i): The derivative of $f(x)$ is

$$f'(x) = 6x - 2.$$

Step (ii): Putting $f'(x) = 0$ gives

$$6x - 2 = 0,$$

which has solution

$$x = \tfrac{1}{3}.$$

Step (iii): The value of $f(x)$ at this point is

$$f(\tfrac{1}{3}) = 3 \times (\tfrac{1}{3})^2 - 2 \times \tfrac{1}{3} + 5 = 4\tfrac{2}{3}.$$

Step (iv): The values of $f(x)$ at the end-points $x = -1$ and $x = 4$ are

$$f(-1) = 3 \times (-1)^2 - 2 \times (-1) + 5 = 10$$

and

$$f(4) = 3 \times 4^2 - 2 \times 4 + 5 = 45.$$

Step (v): The lowest value of $f(x)$ within the given range is $4\tfrac{2}{3}$ (at the stationary point $x = \tfrac{1}{3}$).

(b) The given function is

$$f(t) = 6 + 4t - t^2 \quad (-1 \le t \le 1).$$

Step (i): The derivative of $f(t)$ is

$$f'(t) = 4 - 2t.$$

Step (ii): Putting $f'(t) = 0$ gives

$$4 - 2t = 0,$$

whose solution is

$$t = 2.$$

Step (iii): There is no need to evaluate $f(2)$, because $t = 2$ is outside the range of values given for t. So there are no turning points inside this range, and the lowest point within the range must be at one of the two end-points of the given interval.

Step (iv): The values of $f(t)$ at the end-points $t = -1$ and $t = 1$ are

$$f(-1) = 6 + 4 \times (-1) - (-1)^2 = 1$$

and

$$f(1) = 6 + 4 \times 1 - 1^2 = 9.$$

Step (v): The lowest value of $f(t)$ within the given range is 1 (at $t = -1$).

(c) The given function is

$$f(y) = ay^2 + by + c \quad \left(-\frac{b}{a} \le y \le 0\right),$$

where a and b are positive constants and c is a constant.

Step (i): The derivative of $f(y)$ is

$$f'(y) = 2ay + b.$$

Step (ii): Putting $f'(y) = 0$ gives

$$2ay + b = 0,$$

and the solution of this equation is

$$y = -\frac{b}{2a}.$$

Step (iii): The value of $f(y)$ at this point is

$$f\left(-\frac{b}{2a}\right) = a\left(-\frac{b}{2a}\right)^2 + b\left(-\frac{b}{2a}\right) + c$$

$$= \frac{b^2}{4a} - \frac{b^2}{2a} + c$$

$$= -\frac{b^2}{4a} + c.$$

Step (iv): The values of $f(y)$ at the end-points $y = -b/a$ and $y = 0$ are

$$f\left(-\frac{b}{a}\right) = a\left(-\frac{b}{a}\right)^2 + b\left(-\frac{b}{a}\right) + c$$

$$= \frac{b^2}{a} - \frac{b^2}{a} + c = c$$

and

$$f(0) = c.$$

Step (v): Because a and b are both positive, the lowest value of $f(y)$ within the given range is

$$-\frac{b^2}{4a} + c,$$

which occurs at the stationary point $y = -b/(2a)$.

Solution 5.7

As in the Solution to Activity 5.2(a), the derivative of

$$f(x) = 3x^2 - 2x + 5$$

is

$$f'(x) = 6x - 2,$$

which gives a single stationary point (solution of $f'(x) = 0$) at $x = \frac{1}{3}$.

(a) At $x = 0$, the value of the derivative is

$$f'(0) = 0 - 2 = -2,$$

which is negative. At $x = 1$, its value is

$$f'(1) = 6 \times 1 - 2 = 4,$$

which is positive. Hence the gradient is negative for $x < \frac{1}{3}$, zero at $x = \frac{1}{3}$ and positive for $x > \frac{1}{3}$. According to the First Derivative Test, this corresponds to a local minimum, as illustrated in Figure 5.5(b).

(b) The second derivative of $f(x)$ is

$$f''(x) = 6,$$

which is positive for all values of x, including $x = \frac{1}{3}$. Hence this stationary point is a local minimum, according to the Second Derivative Test.

Solution 5.8

There are various different ways of expressing the purpose of the model. The three essential points to build into the statement are:

(i) the age of car to buy;

(ii) costs to be kept as low as possible;

(iii) car to be owned for one year.

The following statement is one way of specifying the purpose.

> To determine the age of the chosen type of car to buy, such that the costs of owning and running it for one year are to be as low as possible.

Solution 5.9

The gradient is about 350 and the intercept on the vertical axis is at about 150, which means that a suitable equation is

$$R = 150 + 350A,$$

where R and A have the meanings defined in the text. As values of R are given for values of A between 0 and 6, suitable limitations on the use of this equation would be $0 \le A \le 6$.

Solution 5.10

A suitable list of assumptions is as follows:

(i) that neither the tax and insurance costs nor the petrol costs depend on the age of the car;

(ii) that the repair and maintenance costs increase linearly with the age of the car;

(iii) that the depreciation costs decrease exponentially with the age of the car;

(iv) that the data obtained are applicable to the car which Jim will buy;

(v) that Jim does in fact keep the car for one year.

Solution 5.11

(a) The total cost is just the sum of all the component costs, that is,

$$C = D + R + T + P.$$

Now we have

$$D = 2500 \exp(-0.25A) \quad (0 \le A \le 6)$$

and

$$R = 150 + 350A \quad (0 \le A \le 6),$$

so that the required expression for C is

$$C = 2500 \exp(-0.25A) + 150$$
$$+ 350A + T + P \quad (0 \le A \le 6).$$

(b) Find the value of A which minimises C.

Solution 5.12

We apply the Optimisation Procedure of page 58 to the function given by

$$C = 2500 \exp(-0.25A) + 150$$
$$+ 350A + T + P \quad (0 \le A \le 6).$$

Step (i): The derivative of C with respect to A is

$$\frac{dC}{dA} = 2500 \times (-0.25) \exp(-0.25A) + 350$$
$$= -625 \exp(-0.25A) + 350 \quad (0 \le A \le 6).$$

Notice that, because T and P do not depend on A, they are treated as constants in the differentiation process and so each has zero derivative.

Step (ii): The equation $dC/dA = 0$ is

$$-625 \exp(-0.25A) + 350 = 0.$$

From this we obtain

$$\exp(-0.25A) = \tfrac{350}{625} = \tfrac{14}{25}$$

or, equivalently,

$$\exp(0.25A) = \tfrac{25}{14}.$$

The solution of this equation is

$$A = 4 \ln(\tfrac{25}{14}) = 2.32,$$

to three significant figures. This value is within the stated limits for A.

Step (iii): When A has this value, we find that

$$C = 2500 \times \tfrac{14}{25} + 150 + 350 \times 4 \ln(\tfrac{25}{14}) + T + P$$
$$= 2360 + T + P,$$

to three significant figures.

Step (iv): When $A = 0$, we have

$$C = 2500 \exp 0 + 150 + 0 + T + P$$
$$= 2650 + T + P.$$

When $A = 6$, we have

$$C = 2500 \exp(-0.25 \times 6) + 150 + 350 \times 6 + T + P$$
$$= 2810 + T + P,$$

to three significant figures.

Step (v): The smallest value of C is at the stationary point, when $A = 2.32$ (to three significant figures).

Solution 5.13

It is necessary to recall both what A represents and the original question. The modelling assumptions should also be borne in mind.

The nature of these assumptions means that the predicted value of A will not be very accurate. Hence even two significant figures may be too many for the final answer. A reasonable recommendation to Jim might be to buy a car that is about two to two and a half years old.

Solutions to Exercises

Solution 3.1

Each of the derivatives below is obtained by using one of the entries in Table 3.2 on page 38, the Constant Multiple Rule or the Sum Rule.

(a) Since $\sqrt{t} = t^{1/2}$, we have

$$f(t) = t^2\sqrt{t} = t^{5/2} \quad (t > 0).$$

The derivative of this is

$$f'(t) = \tfrac{5}{2}t^{3/2} \quad (t > 0),$$

which may also be written as

$$f'(t) = \tfrac{5}{2}t\sqrt{t} \quad (t > 0).$$

(b) Since $1/y^3 = y^{-3}$, the derivative of

$$f(y) = \frac{1}{y^3} + \cos(5y) \quad (y > 0)$$

is

$$f'(y) = -3y^{-4} - 5\sin(5y)$$
$$= -\frac{3}{y^4} - 5\sin(5y) \quad (y > 0).$$

(c) The derivative of

$$f(s) = 14\sin\left(\frac{s}{7}\right)$$
$$= 14\sin(\tfrac{1}{7}s)$$

is

$$f'(s) = 2\cos\left(\frac{s}{7}\right).$$

(d) The derivative of

$$f(x) = 3(\exp(5x) - \exp(-5x))$$
$$= 3\exp(5x) - 3\exp(-5x)$$

is

$$f'(x) = 15\exp(5x) + 15\exp(-5x)$$
$$= 15(\exp(5x) + \exp(-5x)).$$

(e) The derivative of

$$f(v) = 2\ln\left(\frac{v}{8}\right)$$
$$= 2\ln(\tfrac{1}{8}v) \quad (v > 0)$$

is

$$f'(v) = \frac{2}{v} \quad (v > 0).$$

Solution 3.2

(a) By expanding the expression given, we obtain

$$f(t) = (t - 1)^3$$
$$= t^3 - 3t^2 + 3t - 1,$$

whose derivative is

$$f'(t) = 3t^2 - 6t + 3$$
$$= 3(t - 1)^2.$$

(b) Recalling that $\exp(p)$ is another way of writing e^p, and applying the law of indices, we have

$$f(z) = \exp(1 + 2z) = e^{1+2z} = e^1 e^{2z}.$$

The derivative is therefore

$$f'(z) = 2e^1 e^{2z} = 2e^{1+2z} = 2\exp(1 + 2z).$$

(c) Using the rule $\ln(p^q) = q\ln p$ for logarithms, we have

$$f(y) = \ln(y^3) = 3\ln y \quad (y > 0),$$

for which the derivative is

$$f'(y) = \frac{3}{y} \quad (y > 0).$$

(d) Using the hint given, we have

$$f(x) = \sin(1 + x) = \sin 1 \cos x + \cos 1 \sin x,$$

whose derivative is

$$f'(x) = -\sin 1 \sin x + \cos 1 \cos x.$$

This may be rewritten as

$$f'(x) = \cos(1 + x).$$

Solution 4.1

In each case, the first derivative is given in the Solution to Exercise 3.1 above. The further differentiations are then carried out using the results of Section 3.

(a) The first derivative is

$$f'(t) = \tfrac{5}{2}t^{3/2} \quad (t > 0),$$

and so the second derivative is

$$f''(t) = \tfrac{5}{2} \times \tfrac{3}{2}t^{1/2}$$
$$= \tfrac{15}{4}t^{1/2} \quad (t > 0),$$

which may also be written as

$$f''(t) = \tfrac{15}{4}\sqrt{t} \quad (t > 0).$$

(b) The first derivative is

$$f'(y) = -3y^{-4} - 5\sin(5y) \quad (y > 0),$$

and so the second derivative is

$$f''(y) = 12y^{-5} - 25\cos(5y)$$
$$= \frac{12}{y^5} - 25\cos(5y) \quad (y > 0).$$

(c) The first derivative is

$$f'(s) = 2\cos\left(\frac{s}{7}\right),$$

and so the second derivative is

$$f''(s) = -\tfrac{2}{7}\sin\left(\frac{s}{7}\right).$$

(d) The first derivative is

$$f'(x) = 15\exp(5x) + 15\exp(-5x),$$

and so the second derivative is

$$f''(x) = 75\exp(5x) - 75\exp(-5x)$$
$$= 75(\exp(5x) - \exp(-5x)).$$

(e) The first derivative is

$$f'(v) = \frac{2}{v} = 2v^{-1} \quad (v > 0),$$

and so the second derivative is

$$f''(v) = -2v^{-2} = -\frac{2}{v^2} \quad (v > 0).$$

Solution 5.1

(a) The derivative of

$$f(x) = 3x^4 - 2x^3 - 9x^2 + 7$$

is

$$f'(x) = 12x^3 - 6x^2 - 18x$$
$$= 6x(2x^2 - x - 3)$$
$$= 6x(x+1)(2x-3).$$

Hence the solutions of $f'(x) = 0$ are

$$x = -1, \quad x = 0 \quad \text{and} \quad x = \tfrac{3}{2}.$$

The corresponding values of $f(x)$ are, respectively,

$$f(-1) = 3, \ f(0) = 7 \text{ and}$$
$$f(\tfrac{3}{2}) = -4\tfrac{13}{16} = -4.8125.$$

The stationary points are therefore at

$$(-1,3), \quad (0,7) \quad \text{and} \quad (\tfrac{3}{2}, -4\tfrac{13}{16}).$$

(b) (i) To apply the First Derivative Test (page 66) to the stationary point at $x = -1$, we calculate the values of $f'(x)$ at $x = -2$ (to the left of $x = -1$) and at $x = -\tfrac{1}{2}$ (to the right of $x = -1$ but to the left of the next stationary point at $x = 0$). Since

$$f'(-2) = -84 < 0 \quad \text{and} \quad f'(-\tfrac{1}{2}) = 6 > 0,$$

the function $f(x)$ has a minimum at $x = -1$ (or at $(-1,3)$).

For the stationary point at $x = 0$, we already know the value of $f'(x)$ at $x = -\tfrac{1}{2}$, which lies to the left of $x = 0$ but to the right of the previous stationary point considered. Evaluating $f'(x)$ also at $x = 1$ (to the right of $x = 0$ but to the left of the next stationary point at $x = \tfrac{3}{2}$), we have

$$f'(-\tfrac{1}{2}) = 6 > 0 \quad \text{and} \quad f'(1) = -12 < 0,$$

showing that the function $f(x)$ has a maximum at $x = 0$ (or at $(0,7)$).

For the stationary point at $x = \tfrac{3}{2}$, we already know the value of $f'(x)$ at $x = 1$, which lies to the left of $x = \tfrac{3}{2}$ but to the right of the previous stationary point considered. Evaluating $f'(x)$ also at $x = 2$ (to the right of $x = \tfrac{3}{2}$), we have

$$f'(1) = -12 < 0 \quad \text{and} \quad f'(2) = 36 > 0,$$

showing that the function $f(x)$ has a minimum at $x = \tfrac{3}{2}$ (or at $(\tfrac{3}{2}, -4\tfrac{13}{16})$).

(ii) The second derivative of the given function $f(x)$ is the derivative of

$$f'(x) = 12x^3 - 6x^2 - 18x,$$

which is

$$f''(x) = 36x^2 - 12x - 18$$
$$= 6(6x^2 - 2x - 3).$$

Now we have

$$f''(-1) = 30 > 0$$

so that, according to the Second Derivative Test on page 67, there is a minimum of $f(x)$ at $x = -1$.

Similarly, since we find

$$f''(0) = -18 < 0,$$

there is a maximum of $f(x)$ at $x = 0$.

From the value

$$f''(\tfrac{3}{2}) = 45 > 0,$$

we deduce that there is a minimum of $f(x)$ at $x = \tfrac{3}{2}$.

Solution 5.2

(a) The velocity $v\,\mathrm{m\,s^{-1}}$ of the ball (measured as positive in the upwards direction) is given by

$$v = \frac{dh}{dt} = 30 - 10t.$$

(b) The ball is projected at time $t = 0$, when its velocity is $30\,\mathrm{m\,s^{-1}}$. The speed is the magnitude of the velocity, so the speed of projection is also $30\,\mathrm{m\,s^{-1}}$.

(c) The ball reaches its maximum height when h is a maximum. From above, we have $dh/dt = 0$ when $t = 3$. This stationary point corresponds to the height

$$h = 30 \times 3 - 5 \times 3^2 = 45,$$

so the ball attains a maximum height of 45 metres. (This is clearly the overall maximum, since it is greater than the zero height at which the ball leaves and returns to its point of projection.)

(d) If $h = 25$, then we have

$$30t - 5t^2 = 25$$

or, on dividing through by 5 and rearranging,

$$t^2 - 6t + 5 = 0.$$

On factorising the left-hand side, this becomes

$$(t - 1)(t - 5) = 0,$$

with solutions $t = 1$ and $t = 5$. Hence the ball is at 25 metres above its point of projection after 1 second and again after 5 seconds. (After 1 second it is on its way up, and after 5 seconds it is falling down.)

Solution 5.3

The equation for the profit, £M, is given by

$$
\begin{aligned}
M &= R - C \\
&= 900 - 600\exp(-5T) - 100 - 180T \\
&= 800 - 600\exp(-5T) - 180T \quad (0 \le T \le 1).
\end{aligned}
$$

The derivative of M with respect to T is

$$\frac{dM}{dT} = 3000\exp(-5T) - 180 \quad (0 \le T \le 1),$$

which is equal to zero when

$$3000\exp(-5T) - 180 = 0.$$

This is equivalent to

$$\exp(-5T) = \frac{180}{3000} = \frac{3}{50},$$

which has solution

$$T = \tfrac{1}{5}\ln\left(\tfrac{50}{3}\right) = 0.563,$$

to three significant figures. This is within the range of values given for T. The corresponding value of M is

$$M = 800 - 36 - 36\ln\left(\tfrac{50}{3}\right) = 663,$$

to three significant figures. This compares with the values $M = 200$ at $T = 0$ and $M = 616$ (to three significant figures) at $T = 1$, so the maximum value of M occurs at the stationary point.

The maximum profit is therefore obtained with a fertiliser application rate of about 0.56 tonnes per hectare. (As the modelling assumptions are not listed, you cannot interpret this result in the light of them, but common sense suggests that an answer given to more than two significant figures is unlikely to be appropriate here.)

Solution 5.4

Using the derivative given in the hint, we have

$$\frac{dF}{dv} = -12\frac{(v^2 - 12)}{(v^2 + 12v + 12)^2} \quad (0 \le v \le 30).$$

This expression is zero when $v^2 - 12 = 0$, that is, when $v = \pm 2\sqrt{3}$. Only the positive value is within the given range of values of v, so we are left with one stationary point to consider at $v = 2\sqrt{3} = 3.46$ (to three significant figures). The corresponding value of F is

$$F = \frac{24\sqrt{3}}{12 + 24\sqrt{3} + 12} = \frac{\sqrt{3}}{1 + \sqrt{3}} = 0.634,$$

to three significant figures.

At $v = 0$ we have $F = 0$, and at $v = 30$ we find

$$F = \frac{12 \times 30}{30^2 + 12 \times 30 + 12} = \frac{360}{1272} = \frac{15}{53} = 0.283,$$

to three significant figures.

So the maximum is attained when $v = 3.46$. This means that the average traffic speed will be about $3.5\,\mathrm{m\,s^{-1}}$ for highest traffic flow. (This speed is not very fast (only about 8 mph), so the traffic planners are unlikely to impose a corresponding speed limit. They might want to revisit the model instead.)